I0734437

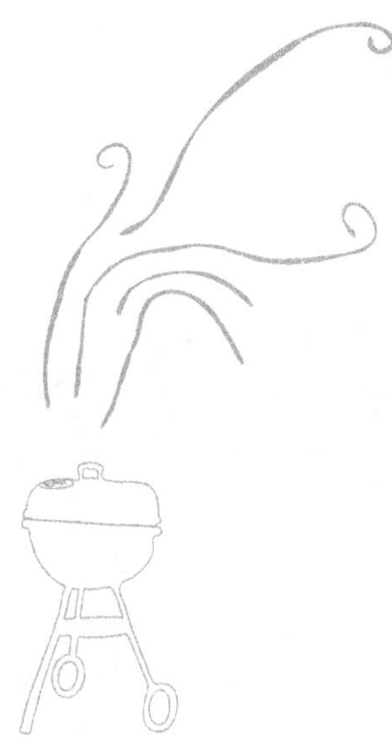

Four Fathers

fiction and poetry

Dave Housley

BL Pawelek

Tom Williams

Ben Tanzer

Cobalt Press

Baltimore, MD

ISBN: 978-1-941462-00-3
Cover and book design by Amanda Gilleland

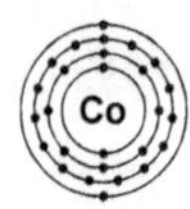

Cobalt Press
Baltimore, MD

www.cobaltpress.org

For all inquiries, including requests for review materials, please contact info@cobaltpress.org.

Foreword

Greg Olear

The *Bible*—of which there is an estimated six billion copies in print—takes great pains to relay the following information: Adam begat Seth begat Enos begat Cainan begat Mahalaleel begat Jared begat Methusaleh begat Lamech begat Noah begat Shem. This genealogical aside is not confined to the Apocrypha, or buried in Psalms. It is placed in the fifth chapter of Genesis, the very first book, right up front.

Understand: for all its ubiquity, we know little definitively about the *Bible*. We don't know when it was written. We don't know where it was written. We don't even know who it was written by. What we do know is that Lamech was Jared's grandson, and not the other way around. Clearly patrilineal pedigree was important to the authors. Whoever they were.

Indeed, fatherhood is the most timeless topic in our literature. The earliest known human writing—as much older than the *Bible* as *What to Expect When You're Expecting* is newer—concerns the parentage of various Sumerian deities, whose claims to absolute power revolved on that eternal question: Who's your daddy? Fatherhood forms a throughline in our great books, from Genesis to *Hamlet* to *Shit My Dad Says*. Nothing is more elemental.

And yet nothing so old is more changed, and thus fraught with confusion. Since the introduction of the plow until, if we must pick an arbitrary marker, the birth of Frances Bean Cobain, the role of the father has been more or less unchanged in Western society. There were good fathers and rotten ones, sure, but the role of the Old Man was the same. Only with this generation—my generation—have fathers begun to stay at home in large numbers, to more actively care for their children, to *co-parent*—a term that shows just how detached men used to be from the business of raising kids. The whole ballgame is different now. These are not your father's fathers.

The contributors to this remarkable collection, then, are wrestling with themes at once eternal and brand-spanking new. BL Pawelek, Tom Williams, Ben Tanzer, Dave Housley: four fathers writing in four different forms—poetry, stories, flash fiction, and novella, respectively—take on contemporary fatherhood in all its permutations, from the heavy (sympathizing with dads who take out their families) to the light (Justin Bieber is a really stupid name), and everything in between. These writerly dads reveal not only where we should be, but where we are.

Four Fathers

Where You Should Be

Tom Williams

For my father

I

Look, James! There he is—just another office worker streaming out of the double doors of downtown buildings—your very own father.

Impossible. Over eight hundred miles separate you. He and your mother have already spent their annual weekend with their only son, this time in Memphis, your home of eight months. Surely you will blink and discover a fading apparition brought on by stress and the setting sun of a summer's day. Or find a man resembling your father, the same medium-length afro, steel-rimmed glasses and wide, shining brown face, but not your progenitor. Uncanny, you'll tell yourself, then walk to your Audi and drive home, where, certainly, a drink awaits. Yet, as he advances, dressed for July in a tan tropical weight suit, his stride compact in a crowd but powerful nonetheless, this figure doesn't vanish or slowly reveal the features—longer ears, lighter complexion, a tighter mouth—that convince you you're not twenty feet away from the man whose lectures about firm handshakes, crisp diction and cologne you started ignoring in your teens, lest his voice find residence inside your head.

So you stand, immobile as a lamppost, on the corner of Jefferson and Second. As he nears, recall the last phone conversation with your mother, not with him. The longest you and your father have spoken on the phone was fifteen minutes, an argument over a loan he would not give. Your mother said, since his retirement, your father seemed restless, as if tending his vegetable garden and playing racquetball twice a week had lost their charms. Could this restlessness manifest in his leaving suburban Chicagoland and shooting down I-55 on a Thursday? Is his next step to seize your shoulder with his massive mocha fist and say, "Surprise!"

Unlikely. Your father has never been a man given to the impromptu gesture. He's never drunkenly told co-workers at a party in Denver that he'd always loved the home of the blues, then quit his job of twenty-two months and left for Memphis. Thanks to your mother, who's not only white but Scotch/Irish on one side, Finnish on the other, few would suspect, should you and your father stand together, that the two of you are even related. Still, as grumbling pedestrians shoulder past you, the man gets closer. He's definitely smiling, his face brightening and opening in a way yours never does. You prepare for what might happen next while telling yourself this simply cannot be. It can't be him. He gets nearer, raises his hand. You become more aware of the heat, the sweat that slips down your sides like condensation on a bottle of beer, wondering what words you'll use to greet him, if you'll have time to speak before he wraps you up in a brief but forceful hug that will make you feel you haven't grown older than eleven, that your slim body is still at the mercy of his linebacker's arms and broad, muscled chest. And then the man steps past you, opens his arms and embraces the dazzling Indian woman standing slightly to your left.

You stare at this couple for a moment. The man turns in profile and you see on his cheek a birthmark, slightly lighter than his skin and shaped like Portugal. It's not him. You're free to do as you please. And yet you, James Arthur Robinson, cannot move a step.

This has never happened before. You've been in downtown Memphis with your father before, but on that occasion you two toured Beale Street with your mother, the afternoon spoiled when the conversation turned to your many abrupt moves, which number five in ten years since graduation. Your father said, for the third year in a row, that this inability to settle down was a sign of immaturity, while you countered that you hadn't found the place where you *should* be. Yet that predictable drama—concluded only when your mother asked for peace—seems preferable to today's sudden appearance, this hallucination. That's what you call it when you realize your legs and feet can still move, that's what you're fairly sure of when you find your Audi in the parking lot. Now that it's over, though, you don't want it to happen again. Trouble is, as you have no idea how it occurred in the first place, prevention seems well out of your reach.

The drive home is almost entirely devoted to these concerns. In your driveway, you scarcely recall the traffic lights, turns and lane changes that brought you to your townhouse in Midtown—a rental, a waste of money, your father asserts, as he has with all your temporary abodes. Inside, you walk cautiously, as if some other specters lurk in dark corners. You consider calling home but wouldn't know what to say if your father answers. Soon, in the cool of shadow and powerful air conditioning, your powers of detection are exhausted, and you turn to a solution on which you often rely: the mixing of a potent cocktail. Today's choice is a tall plastic tumbler with a thin layer of crushed ice, topped by equal portions of Jim Beam and Coke, which begins its magic directly, easing your mind into a steady and quieting repose. The second tumbler holds less Coke and finds you warm-limbed on the couch before the TV. The third forces laughter even at the most inane sitcoms, while the fourth accompanies you to bed.

Come morning, though, you're startled out of sleep by a dream in which you're again at Jefferson and Second, only now your father possesses ragged claws at the end of block-length arms, and you can't get your feet moving to outrun him. Unfortunately, it's five in the morning, too close to your six o'clock alarm to get back to sleep, so you untangle your legs from the bedclothes, see you're still wearing the pants from last night. You set your feet on the floor but can barely keep your swollen head on your slumping shoulders. This might be a time to call in sick, yet there's a presentation for clients at ten and you're in charge of it. As well, despite the dampness of your brain, you know there are people at the office—in particular, men your age—who might fathom your malady, if that's what it is, and supply you with the remedy. A hot shower and three cups of Colombian scald you into action.

The knot you shape for your tie—without a mirror, no less—might compensate for the uneven shave from your Remington. You guardedly make your way outside, finding no fathers behind hedges or in the shadows of the carport or back seat. Nor does he drive beside you on Poplar or greet you at the counter of Krystal. All the way to your office you encounter faces, but none gives you pause. You remain wary, though, sensing this experience is not at all over.

There's no time to fret at work. The presentation can't be postponed. Yet you're not worried, because you've always been able to sell yourself and the marketing capacities of whoever is employing you with the barest preparation. In a way you owe this to none other than your father.

Once you realized all his professional advice wasn't about acting *white,* as your adolescent self suspected, you determined that dear old dad was telling you what whites, with their lifetime of privilege, demanded and expected from the few minorities they were willing to let aboard. And now you feel fully armed with their secrets, knowing what clients want to hear and how they want to hear it said. Today's speech is seamless, on point and comic at the right times. You almost believe in the deferential and humble nature you ascribe to yourself and Malik and Justin, your co-presenters. You respond to all questions in an efficient manner that assumes and answers follow-ups before they're asked. For only one moment you are a little oblique—a five-second fugue where you contemplate the features of your father's face, hazily superimposed over the massive clock. But two blinks later, you can see straight again.

Afterward, in the break room, where you think your coffee could use a splash of cream and another of Old Granddad, you're congratulated by co-workers who heard about the presentation, everyone certain Mother's Frozen Biscuit Dough will employ Pratt and Loomis as their next marketing firm. While Justin and Malik stand by accepting praise, you size them up as quality subjects to ask about recent visual phenomena. Though, individually, each is nothing like you (has anyone ever been, James?), both are around your age—thirty-two—and they share your cultural experience and genetic information: Justin has a Jewish mother and Presbyterian father; Malik is suburban and African-American. You're slightly unnerved by the conditions of their shirtfronts and suits—starched and spotless—especially when compared to your stains and wrinkles, but before you can say a word, Justin invites you to a celebratory lunch.

Soon you're out of the office and riding the trolley to North Main, exiting right in front of Dewey's, a noisy tavern that serves dripping burgers, crisp fries and tall drafts. You order the largest draft they've got and grab the twenty-four ouncer with both hands. For ten or fifteen minutes, the chatter is dominated by Justin and Malik and strictly in-house: clients and their demands, is their boss, Alan, leaving for a rival firm, does the new receptionist resemble Gwyneth Paltrow. You participate minimally, gulp down your beer, order another, willing yourself not to look at the nearly full twelve-ounce glasses before your companions, then order a bowl of chili to demonstrate you also eat on occasion. "Thirsty, huh," Justin says, one hand covering the top of his mug.

You nod, look around at the waitresses in shorts and tank tops, then at the customers, most of them white, professional men. In one sweeping glance, you see no one who looks like your father, yet at each turn you detect a gesture or a quality that reminds you of him: erect posture, ear cocked to listen better, booming laughter at maudlin jokes, sleeves rolled in perfect cuffs, shoes buffed to a mirror-like sheen. Absently, your free hand touches the excellent knot in your tie, but you loosen it as if to reveal how James Arthur Robinson—biracial, anti-social, iconoclastic—is so unlike those gathered here, as if to demonstrate that you definitely didn't learn how to tie a double-Windsor at the master bathroom mirror, your father behind you manipulating your hands.

Now you turn to Malik and Justin, such an unlikely pair yet each a native Memphian who commutes from the 'burbs after a two-mile jog. Both are handsome—Malik with his smooth, shaven head and well-trimmed mustache, Justin with slate-gray eyes, dimples and a cleft chin—and exude an air of confidence scented by Ralph Lauren or Calvin Klein.

Their addresses don't change every two years. They regularly vote. Wedding rings sit prominently on their fingers, the skin beneath pale, even on Malik, who's two shades darker than you but has been married ten years. You'd pose them in an ad for a company asserting diversity along with rectitude and virtue. Come now, James: How can you ask if they're anything like you?

After another sloshing swallow, you take the best method and plunge:

"Either of you ever see your father, I don't know, where he wouldn't ordinarily be?"

A second passes, maybe two. You wish for some remote control button to rewind and erase the previous moment, certain the looks crossing their faces will reveal absolute stupefaction. But both men look at one another, then start laughing. You gulp more beer, gauging if you should order another so the third arrives as you're finishing your second. Should you have a third, James?

Then Malik says, "You see that guy, too?"

"What?" They can't be talking about the man you saw yesterday. They don't know your father. You never brought him into the office. The only photos you own are at home, face-down in a kitchen drawer beneath matchbooks and coasters from local bars.

"That comic," Justin says. "On Letterman last night. What was his name?" He pounds the table lightly with his fist. The food arrives, brought by a blonde who looks harried by flirtatious businessmen. You start to order another draft, think better of it. Malik says, "I think it was Cruz. Somebody Cruz." He bites his pickle spear, points the remaining half at you. "I thought you didn't watch that show."

You quit watching Letterman after he left NBC. The show's as ordinary as oatmeal, which is evidenced by well meaning but utterly unoriginal folk like Malik and Justin tuning in nightly. "I wasn't," you begin, but Justin interrupts:

"I laughed my ass off. Because it's so damned true."

"Woke up the kids I was laughing so hard," Malik says. The memory is humorous enough to make him laugh again. Justin joins him in the mirth. Even you force a dry chuckle, though you have no idea why.

Justin says, "Yeah. I saw my dad this morning."

"You did?" you say, a trifle baffled.

Hasn't Justin spoken of his parents' retirement home in Ft. Meyers?

"Where?"

Justin doesn't speak. He gestures to Malik, who says, "Same place I saw mine."

Now you're really confused, as you know Malik's folks live in upstate Michigan during the hot months.

Again, you say, "Where?"

"You didn't see Letterman?" Justin says, reaching for his fries.

You shake your head.

"He doesn't know the joke," Malik says, looking at Justin.

"What joke?" you say, exasperated and staring at an empty glass.

Together, Justin and Malik say, "In the mirror while I was shaving." Again, they erupt into laughter, Malik even slapping the table a few times. The waitress reappears but you wave her away. "What do you mean?" you say.

Slightly composed, Justin says, "I can't remember if his first name was Cruz or his last."

"Last," Malik says.

“Jesus,” you say. “What are you two talking about?”

“You don’t get it?” Justin says. “You look in the mirror one morning and you see your father there?”

Your subsequent silence causes concern. Malik leans forward. “Come on, bro,” he says. “We’re all getting a little older. Starting to look like the old man.”

“So you see him instead of you in the mirror,” Justin says, his words as deliberate as if he were speaking to a foreigner.

“Oh,” you say, leaning back and clutching your empty glass against your torso. Your tie dampens, but you overlook it. The joke is kind of funny, in a lightweight and commonplace way. But the bigger joke is you looking in any mirror and seeing your father. Your narrow face isn’t the same shape. You’re three shades lighter. Your goddamned eyes are blue! The relative you resemble most is your mother’s father, who spoiled you rotten but never called your father by his name. His is not a face you want to see, even in dreams.

Now, while you dig a spoon into your tepid chili, Malik and Justin confer over the comedian’s name. Soon, the conversation returns to office business. Justin’s sure the boss is leaving, Malik isn’t, but you’re too disinterested to mediate. After divvying up the check, you leave five more to cover your tab, consider stopping at the bar for a quick shot or two, but Justin and Malik step toward the door, open it a crack to check on the heat, then you follow them outside, only to just avoid bumping into someone. When you look up to apologize, your mouth opens but seizes shut when you see your father an arm’s length away.

Again, it wasn’t him. The man’s hair was as silvery, but he was a full five inches taller, and his cologne smelled dearer than English Leather, without which your father never went anywhere. At home, late Friday, you scold yourself, still embarrassed how you tripped over Justin trying to avoid the man, who took one disapproving look at you—increasing his resemblance to *you know who*—then ventured inside. Tonight you’re not bothering with the Coke and occasionally foregoing the tumbler.

On one hand, you’re clinging to the notion that the second hallucination was brought on by the drinks. That and all the banter about fathers. On the other hand, you still can't explain the first sighting and the subsequent dream. You're stuck with jokes as a poor explanation. Even though it's no longer that funny, you ponder the coincidence of this comic's appearance on the same night of your first experience. It seems evidence of a conspiracy, paternal forces managing to bring together men of various races and backgrounds, but even you can't swallow that whopper. Now you wish you'd asked Justin and Malik—or this Cruz fellow—what they felt when they saw on the other side of the mirror their father's face. An initial shock of growing old, you're sure, such as that attending the discovery of a sleep line that doesn't smooth out after the morning's ablutions. You shave with the Remington to avoid mirrors. What's reflected there is too often a surprise—especially after a rough night—and you don't need any more than you already have.

But did Justin and Malik also feel joy? Sure, they speak of their fathers with the occasional condemnation and distaste one commonly hears, yet, unlike you, they actually speak of their fathers, gladly spend time with them. As the bourbon stings your gums, you suspect these men were happy to see the old man grinning through a face covered in shaving cream. Surely over them came a sense of accomplishment, whereas you don't know what any of this means. You're sure they're a sign—these dreams and visions—but of what? The importance of cologne? You never wear it, in part because everyone else does, but also because your father claimed it was a necessity for him and for you. Once, while emptying into his palms a bottle of English Leather (a full bottle perched in his medicine chest), he said, "They think we smell bad." You knew who *they* and *we* were when you said, "We don't." But your father, smoothing his hands over his neck, chest and arms, said, "Of course, that doesn't stop them from checking." He reached out to you with his hand, but you pulled away. You'd show him he was wrong. Wouldn't you?

The weekend passes, for the most part, uneventfully, as does the following week. However, there are enough uncertainties and curiosities to convince you the period you've reached does not designate an end to this odyssey. The TV, for one, long a friend to have a few with, produces a few odd moments. For most of your life, the screen hasn't bustled with black faces and never showed a face like yours. You remember the thrill of seeing Nipsey Russell or Della Reese on *Password,* even though they'd be replaced in a week by McLean Stevenson and Betty White. But either your present vision is so father-oriented or some conspiracy is at play: Sunday, your father discusses affirmative action with Mike Wallace; Tuesday he's analyzing the batting strokes of the Braves; Thursday he pulls double duty as a bassist behind Pete Townshend and an angry, semi-literate father of an injured son on an emergency room drama. That you've even landed on that program long enough to watch is unbelievable, considering how much you loathe any series popular with the masses you're paid to manipulate. And though you know you really saw a Georgetown Law professor, Joe Morgan, a British musician and a SAG member, you aren't thrilled that you thought they each resembled your father. For isn't that a short step from the perception that blacks all look alike, James? And isn't that evidence that you, light enough to pass if you ever wanted, are angry at the man directly responsible for the darker part of you?

Yet you loved his brothers, those easy-going uncles who worked in factories or collected unemployment, who told off-color stories in loud voices while lighting up Kools and crushing malt liquor cans. They never gave advice about scrubbing vigorously underneath your arms or always walking behind a superior. Then again, you only saw them once every few months, and they were, according to your cousins, not the best providers or role models. All your cousins envied you your father: his bankroll and education, the stability and direction he gave you. Whenever you complained or wished aloud for him to change, your cousins looked to one another like veterans of an unpopular war, then hissed that you had it made.

Meanwhile, you achieve a temporary stopgap: no more TV. On the sidewalks and behind the wheel and even in your office, you'll try not to look at faces. Keep your eyes level. Avoid lures to look up. That might help. Oh yes, there are also drinks. There are a lot of them, James, but enough to quiet the squabble in your head?

Your name, you know, is a common one. A look in the phonebook would reveal, in Shelby County alone, two pages of Robinsons. And in every town you've lived you've answered the phone and said yes, you were James Robinson, but discovered you weren't the one the caller was looking for. So it shouldn't surprise you to hear, on Friday, a voice calling "Jimmy," over and over. You needn't even feel compelled to answer, as you're a block away from your building, and everyone there calls you James. In fact, that you are walking along under a blue umbrella against the rain, you must be fairly narcissistic to feel singled out as the Jimmy being addressed by this unknown speaker. Keep walking, James. It's likely to be somebody shouting into his cell. No reason to pause, no reason to turn around, no need to wipe your face as if to remove any obstacle between your eyes and the people around you.

Yet why does the voice keep calling? Why does no one answer? Why does the voice take on a deep timbre and exasperation that reminds you of a day you were cutting the grass, your hearing lulled by the drone of the motor, the racket of cicadas and the competing music of birdsong, while your eleven-year-old body loosened under the sun? You were daydreaming of an invention that would make this onerous task easier: a remote control mower, piloted with one lazy finger from the shade of the porch, chewing up the half-acre suburban lawn into microscopic bits that made raking unnecessary, too. You heard your name then, heard it as if you were underwater and unable to measure the distance between you and the person calling. And then, as sharp as if it was shouted in your ear—which it was—you heard "Jimmy" and, startled, you shut off the mower, turned around, and saw your father, fists dug into his hips, his white shirt dramatically highlighting the depth of his skin color, and the look on his face one of concern and displeasure. Close enough to touch, he said nothing. He shook his head and pointed backward to the path you'd taken. You turned to see it, a meandering, occasionally curving swath of grass, cut from, at first, your lawn, but then your neighbors', so far distant from the starting point you couldn't have recreated it if you tried. "Jimmy," he finally said. "You've got to keep your mind together."

Now, beneath the protection of your umbrella, you search the crowd but are not graced by the sight of him, either as the younger man he was then—around your age now—or the man in his late-fifties. The faces are many but none you know. Yet there it is again, the voice calling, "Jimmy, Jimmy." You turn this way and that, then start running. The voice doesn't dim, though it doesn't get nearer. You make it across the street to your parking lot, where you fumble with the keys like a victim in a slasher movie, then, at last, get in and start your Audi. The engine sputters and you press too hard on the accelerator, forcing out a roar that causes other patrons to stare. You steer forward, drive thought the lot, narrowly avoiding bumpers and fenders. Even with the windows shut, you still hear it: "Jimmy, Jimmy." You turn on the radio, yank the volume knob, and get some interference between you and your name. The blast of the AC blower helps, too, and when you're driving down Second, the voice finally ceases. But that doesn't keep you from speeding home to find shelter behind latched windows and locked doors.

Is this where it happened? You examine that Saturday afternoon of the past. A moment out of many, but one so illustrative, so clear, so emblematic of all that distances the two of you today. When your father stood there that afternoon, he must have heard you apologize. He watched as you rolled the mower back to where you began, and he stayed while you pulled the starter cord. "Don't let it snap back so fast," he ordered, then put his hands on yours to position them correctly on the push handle. He watched as you went up one length of the lawn, back, then started your next row. After shouting for you to overlap your rows so as not to leave any stray blades and patches, he walked toward the house, his head noticeably shaking back and forth. You could still feel the weight of his hands on yours. He was disappointed, you knew that, and you were briefly embarrassed, but that chill in your stomach warmed into anger, as you overlooked your own errors and relished the knowledge then that he was never happy with you because he was a tyrant, a taskmaster, impossible to please. You had done nothing wrong. Over the evening's penultimate Jim Beam and ice, you wonder what he thought of you then. Did he believe he'd always have to look after you to ensure you didn't push life's mowers continuously off track? Was he preparing to sound a perpetual warning? As you know you can't explain the circumstances of late with rational discussion, you easily slide—especially after a few toddies—into the realm of the irrational. And, while there, it seems your father is not unlike Hamlet's murdered father, materializing in various forms to call your attention to some event requiring action. Or are you looking at it too selfishly, James, that rather than calling for you to watch out for yourself, he's calling for you to come to him?

The drinks make things muddier, filled with so many possibilities you can't find your way through. As you empty the bottle, there's one thing you're certain of: this is happening to no one else and has never happened before. This time, you're the pioneer, and you must live through this and leave a trail behind for those who will follow.

After Saturday's morning visit to the liquor store on Madison, you sit on the edge of your couch with the phone on your trembling legs, unable to make the call. A drink can't hurt, so three seems a good start, and as the last shot swirls down your throat your trembling fingers start punching digits. You've never programmed your parents' number into the phone's memory. While it's ringing, you pour another drink, swallow half the contents in time to hear your mother answer. Rare is hers the first voice you hear.

Typically, your father answers after one ring only to say, "Let me get your mother." Today, though, it's Mom, happy to hear from you. She asks what you're doing this weekend, and you consider telling her the truth, but the second swallow that empties your fourth shot tells you to speak of what else is on your table: the minutiae of work. Which is, to some extent, the truth, as Monday morning promises another presentation, before a set of clients flying in from Nashville. Either this account sufficiently bores her or you're incoherent, because she says, "Well, what else is going on?"

"Not much," you say, pouring another. You dash the whole drink and say what you've been meaning to: "Is Dad there?" You await her answer, pour another for the confidence you'll need to keep from stammering when he's on the other end, so you can say "Did I let you down?" or "What the fuck did you want from me?"

"He's not here," your mother says.

This statement shouldn't affect you so harshly, James. Still, you spill a good portion of your bourbon on your shirt, then stand and say, "Where is he?" You look around the living room wildly, as if he's got you right were he wants you, completely vulnerable to whatever he plans. Your free hand wipes at the stain on your shirt, as your mother says, "He's just run over to the grocery store. He'll be back in a few minutes."

"Oh," you say, suddenly slumping, as if the wires producing your antic motion have snapped.

"What did you want to talk to him about?" your mother says, obvious cheer in her voice.

You shake your head, aware now of the effect so many shots in a short span can have on a person. "Nothing," you say, trying to think of an end to this conversation. You don't have call waiting and don't like to lie to your mother, but there is the matter of Monday's presentation, so you mention that again and say goodbye. Once the receiver's in the cradle, you've got both hands free. You reach again for the bottle but take one more wary look around you, then watch the bourbon splash into the bottom of the glass.

When the phone rings next, you're awakened and wondering if it's your father, curious to know why you asked for him. But the voice on the other end is Justin's, and while he's not frantic, he sounds concerned as he says,

"I thought we were going to huddle before the presentation?"

Once your mouth begins working, you say, "Sure, Monday morning."

There's silence for a few seconds, until Justin whispers, "It is Monday."

"Is this another joke from Letterman?" you say, stirring in the bed to see your t-shirt and jeans from Saturday still on and your bare feet coated in dried blood. The bottle you remember emptying is joined by the shattered remains of others and you dive over to the nightstand. Your calendar watch, which you took off on Friday, is the only means of ascertaining if Justin's joking, but it confirms he's telling the truth, along with another key detail: it's eight-forty five. The presentation's scheduled for nine-thirty. "Jesus," you say. "I'll be there." And you toss the receiver, too harried to bother with hanging it up. The drive downtown's only fifteen minutes but that's on a good day. The way things have been lately, you can't depend on the fair light of fortune or even agreeable traffic lights.

A blackout. That's new. But you've no time to reflect on this development. There's time to dress, grab your Remington. Wrigley's might mask breath that probably reeks like a busted fridge. If you'd have listened to your father, you'd have among your emergency auto supplies a bottle of cologne, a mini toothbrush and toothpaste. Then again, if you heeded his advice, you'd not be in Memphis, on your fifth job, and you'd be putting ten percent of your paycheck into mutual funds, another ten into bonds.

When you enter the office, chewing gum like a little leaguer, you see Justin looking at his watch and Malik pointing to the clock, yet they smile and laugh, as you've managed to arrive with fifteen minutes to spare. Trouble is, as you look through the windows of Meeting Room A, you see your boss, Alan, seated with five white men around the table: the Nashville clients, arrived a mite early. Doubtlessly, none of them fears he displays the clear signs of alcoholism. They sit there, smooth peach and pale faces, their dark suits and white shirts as unadorned and austere as the Baptists they probably are. But you can't remember what product they manufacture or the reason why they've left their fair city to hear what the firm of Pratt and Loomis has to say. You grab a coffee and join Malik and Justin. "Man," Malik says. "Have a rough one last night?"

"The flu," you nimbly lie. "Just getting over it." For a moment you feel impressed by the efficiency of your dishonesty, but the smirks crossing both Justin and Malik's lips assure you're mistaken. "I'll handle the pitch," Justin says, blinking and stroking his chin. Another first for today, as, following orders, they always leave the pitch to you. "Malik, you've got Power Point?" Justin says.

Malik nods, turns to you. You examine the pair, their erect postures, well-pressed suits, then touch your tie, drawing attention, you hope, to its shapely knot, as if that might overshadow your otherwise shabby appearance. Justin says, "And you can help us out if they have questions."

"You can be there for moral support," Malik says, rubbing the smooth crown of his head. You nod, sip your coffee. It's as hot as you can stand, yet it doesn't burn away the coating on your tongue.

Inside Meeting Room A, you shake hands with the Nashvilleans, noting how automatically they grip your weak, sweaty palm with strong, dry fingers. Alan eyes you, winding his Rolex, while you get seated between two clients, each with some obscure pin on his lapel. Your father counseled you join some organization—Jaycees, Lions, Optimists—for that's how one made the professional connections he'd need in life. You've never lived long enough in one place to join. Two months shy of three years in Houston is your longest stay anywhere since the nine semesters it took to graduate from Illinois State—instead of Illinois, your father's alma mater. But you left Texas for more money and distractions in Seattle, where only seven months passed before a rival firm's offer ushered you to the Twin Cities, which started out with promise—as all new places do. However, after two dark winters you got tangled with your boss's martini-loving, barely eighteen stepdaughter to relieve the monotony of unremitting snow. Leaving for Denver and yet another new job seemed the only way out, as well as a second chance, but not quite two years later you were recognizing—ten drinks into the evening—how James Robinson, so out of step with the healthy and normal citizens of Colorado, such a sad, lonesome case, belonged where the blues were born. Once you thought that, you were already on your way out again.

Now Justin stands and welcomes the clients with manufactured cheer, and you feel as though, despite an auspicious beginning, this day might not be on a collision course for disaster—a new reason to follow that old pattern of packing up for the next place in line. You're glad when Justin says how happy Pratt and Loomis is to have the men from Fahr's Snack Foods here, as you can quit trying to recall just what it is they make. For now you confirm they are all Baptists or fundamentalists of some sort, as what makes Fahr's stand out is their custom of printing Bible verses on the back of each bag. If you could choose clients, you'd pass up these clowns. Their product tastes like cardboard, even to one with as few remaining taste buds as yourself. Worse, you think it smarmy and superior to stamp "And God so loved the world" on a bag of pizza-flavored pork rinds, as if to suggest their fried pigskin will ensure one's eternal reward.

Yet you don't think about this for long, nor do you linger in worry over your father-obsession and the missing hours from your weekend. You try to focus on Justin and Malik, who ably directs the PowerPoint demonstration. Soon, Justin brings his pitch to a close, the last images leave the screen. Bodies settle into chairs, stomachs gurgle, throats are cleared, and someone's sniffing. Right next to you. You think he was introduced as the VP of something or other, a pinkish man with small hands and rat-like features. You can't tell if he's suffering from an onset of flu or if he's smelling something. In your peripheral vision, you're sure you see him lean back, as if to get away from the source of the stench. Pick one, James: is it your unwashed feet or your fetid armpits? You press the inside of your upper arms closer to your trunk to trap the stink while you wish for that emergency bottle of cologne, along with that remote control that allows the errors of life to be erased or reviewed, that non-existent item you've felt an increasing need for lately.

Around the table, the talk continues, but you hear only enough to notice Justin and Malik aren't speaking. Instead, it's the clients, obviously posing tough questions—the ones you're here to answer. The VP next to you is silent, but that must be a defense against the odor exiting your pores with the potency of methane. Your parched mouth opens, but it's not water or coffee you need. You pull away from the VP to your left, only to nearly bump against the fellow on your right, who you hear drawling about the quote-unquote right kind of people. Next voice is Justin's, and, with a tremor and two coughs, he says, "That's something I bet James could answer."

The squeak of seat cushions and the gristly creak of ankles and knees sounds, for the moment, oppressive. You lick but don't wet your lips, then squint though there's no sunlight. You could ask to have the question repeated, but that would be of no use. It would only give you time to explore how empty your head is of any pertinent information regarding Fahr's Snack Foods and what Pratt and Loomis might do for them. Two Fridays ago, you answered every question in a sentence, and the clients were ready to sign contracts by the close of the business day. You prided yourself on your ability to think on your feet—to know precisely how you could help the biscuit dough and snack food manufacturers of the world make the hoi polloi crave their products—but this morning you don't have that and nothing in your reach will secure it. You say, "I'm just going to agree with Justin." Each of your hands holds its partner and you lean back in your chair as far as it will go.

"They think we smell bad," your father said so long ago. What could you say to him now?

Driving home, you don't worry about the weak handshakes and dispirited looks on Malik and Justin's faces at the close of the meeting. You don't fear Alan's request that you set up a time where the two of you can huddle. A threat to get your ass in gear, you're pretty sure, just as you're sure the preachy potato-chip men will still be looking for a new marketing firm. But you needed to get out, so you left, not telling anyone when you'd be back or where you were going. If anyone ponders aloud what is wrong with you, Justin and Malik will eagerly share how you polish off drinks and claim you smelled like a distillery this morning. And they'd be right to conclude that the bags you're thinking of packing should accompany you to a treatment center. You'll concede such a visit is a distinct, perhaps necessary, possibility, but not yet. Not today. There are still some other matters, though no one at the office knows about them. You've never shared. Not here or anywhere.

After you exit the car and walk inside the dark chill of your townhouse, you turn up evidence of your weekend—a *Hustler*, two bags of Fahr's sour-cream and onion chips, an empty Elvis decanter—and shudder to reconstruct the story these disparate pieces form. In the shower, you use up all the hot water in your tank, yet you emerge feeling covered in a tacky film. Still, you keep moving, ignoring empties and stuffing your suitcase with clothes and sundries. The airlines are too expensive, a bus would depress you, and you're not sure where the train depot is. So you've got to drive the 800 miles up I-55 to the house you grew up in. The thirteen hours it will take, you fear, lends many opportunities to turn back, and you can't keep from wishing for some alternative means of travel, a transporter, as in *Star Trek*, a show you hated because everyone else loved it. But you must stop dreaming of inventions yet to be constructed, James. Your transporter, your robotic lawn mower, your remote control. You've got to deal with what's before you, what you can get your hands on. And in this house the only items meeting that criteria, the bottles, are empty. You've used them all up. You must know this.

So you hustle outside and stuff your bags in the Audi quickly as if to not give yourself a moment to hesitate and change your mind. You forget that your father was right when he predicted you'd always pay too much for repairs and service, and that one shouldn't buy an automobile because few others owned them. Now you jab your key at the ignition twice before its teeth find their grooves, then yank out your wallet to make sure you've got your Amex. When you find the green plastic card, your frantic motion stalls, as you realize this is the credit card your father told you to apply for. You have listened to him before, haven't you? You haven't only used his advice as the norm to gleefully deviate from. Once in a while, you've conceded—though never to his face—that you would be well served to move in the direction to which he was pointing. Right now, though, you need to leave Memphis. You can stop sometime before five to call the office and say you need a week off. Whether anyone agrees with you or allows your request doesn't matter. You will head north on I-55 until the landscape becomes familiar. You will exit the interstate and drive through what will certainly be new development in your hometown. You won't stop to investigate old haunts, nor will you pull into a liquor store or carry out for courage, nor will you try to find old friends because you long ago chose not to have any. You'll keep going until you reach the driveway you once hated to shovel. You'll leave your bags inside the Audi, for what really counts is inside the house. If he's not home, you'll kiss your surprised mother and wait. Most likely, he will be there, sweating from hours of yanking weeds or nurturing the tender leaves of carrots. He'll be equally surprised. You'll see it in his face as he searches for what to say. You too will undeniably be at a loss for words, even though you'll have rehearsed what to say during the drive. But you'll have exhausted all your recriminations and will have forgotten all your apologies. It will definitely seem then, as you both stand there, as close as you've been in years, that words aren't what either of you need. You need to embrace him, Jimmy, to have your father in your own hands. You may even kiss him. You won't need to worry about when to let go.

This sounds like a promise. You turn the key.

Puzzles

Ben Tanzer

For the boys: redux, yo.

Consumption

When he says that he wants to eat her fingers, you are aghast and entertained all at once. He is your drinking friend, which is a nice way of saying that you are concerned about his drinking, especially when you are not out together and it is not clear to you that someone will be keeping an eye on him. He gets into fights while waiting in line at the car wash, and, while the people he meets on these lines suddenly find themselves with broken collarbones, you inevitably find yourself serving as a character witness. He is incredibly charming, intelligent, funny, and full of joy. And while he is attractive as hell with his quick smile, thick dark hair and Mexican lineage, he may not be quite as attractive as his sad-eyed Southern Californian beach babe wife. The one he spontaneously married. The one who can wear a tight, faux snakeskin dress like few other women you know, but who seems so unhappy so much of the time, you almost want to laugh to keep from crying. You suppose what you're doing here is presenting just one part of the picture: the part that you think must somehow explain something about his desire to eat her fingers. The part that says he lacks impulse control, that he is someone whose drinking must surely cloud his decision-making skills, and that he has tendencies toward violent resolutions and an inability to love his wife like he believes he might have if they were happier, all of which must surely impact his desires. You should note here that it's not his wife's fingers he wants to eat, but those of his newborn daughter. She who is the color of a latte and so ridiculously full of unrequited love that, when you are around her, you are worried that one of you will surely burst from the sheer cuteness alone. It's her fingers he wants to eat, and that is why you are aghast and entertained all at once. It seems so unreal to you. He wants to eat those little fingers? He wants to somehow damage the perfect entity lying before us?

How can someone feel that way? Here's the thing, though: you are not yet a parent when he says this to you. You do not understand how different that kind of love is, how all-consuming and overwhelming it can feel. How hard it is to not want to merge with them in every possible way, because to not merge is to not live. But you know now. You know the feeling he spoke of, the intensity that comes with their very presence, and the desire to devour your child, because there is so much feeling involved that it takes everything you have not to lose yourself completely in them, much less contain that feeling when someone else you love is around and willing to listen.

Younger

Maybe your dad was right, your wife says as the two of you sit at the kitchen table one Sunday morning, the half-eaten pancakes lying there in a pool of coagulating syrup, *The New York Times* scattered everywhere, the boys off in the back, screaming, crying, shouting, fighting, all of it, and endlessly at that.

You sit there for a moment trying to figure out what your father might have been right about. He was a smart guy and full of unsolicited, though at times useful advice, but what could he have said that applies here, and now?

Yeah, you say, about what, how you should never pee off of the back of a truck into the wind? That was sound advice you think, though clearly stolen from *On the Road*.

Your wife laughs her throaty Brenda Vaccaro laugh. No, that other thing, she says. What, how there's no reason to get married, or how you should always drive defensively, he loved that one, you say.

Nope, she says scanning the Style section, not those either.

There's something else, you think. Fuck, really, what?

Got nothing, you say.

That's what she said, she says.

Indeed, you say, well played. What, then? What are we talking about here?

That thing about how you don't need to have more than one kid, she says, how you, your mom, and him, the three of you, were a good team, but then they added your brother and it was never quite the same after that.

Now it's your turn to laugh.

Oh, that thing, right, he definitely said that. Don't tell my brother though, you say.

And you both laugh.

The two of you were never going to have just one, never, none maybe, but not one. What if he or she died? Then what? You'd have nothing, and nothing after something was not going to work.

You both felt this way, not that you had ever discussed it. Not that you had to. All you had to do was confirm the feeling when you decided to have the first one, its mutuality, and how wrong it sounded said out loud, but how it had to be said anyway.

Yet, you do wonder which part of having the second one she is referring to.

Is it the sudden lack of money, the endless noise, stress, exhaustion, what, all of it, none of it? Whatever, it doesn't matter. It all kind of sucks, and you don't have to ask which part sucks most.

The boys amble into the room.

The older one turns on the computer, some fashion site he loves. He puts on his headphones and tunes you out completely.

The younger one just sort of falls over on the ground and starts talking to himself, though about what you cannot comprehend, and never can. Something Pokemon, you think, but beyond that is unknown to you and anyone else over four years of age.

You think about the day you brought him home, how scary it was even though you had done it before, and yet how unbelievably yummy he was from jump, so yummy that you could just eat him, and would have, all of him, just gulping him whole.

The older has always been harder, beautiful, but twitchy and ready for a fight, the little one though, he's like a donut, a grimy, oozy, sticky, crying powdered donut that you just want to stroke and smell, and curl-up with at every moment possible.

You look at him some more.

You turn away to look at your wife who is staring at him as well, a small smile snaking across her beautiful face.

You then turn to look out the window again and you realize that you can no longer recall what the two of you were talking about before they came in.

Lies

Do you have a moment?

It's your son's teacher, so this can't be good. Now, not good doesn't have to mean bad, but it means something, and you are too tired for something. You just want to do pick-up and get home.

The teacher tells you that your son lied in class. He stood up in front of everyone and told them how your family's dog died after a classmate of his had shared that her dog had died.

But you don't have a dog, do you? the teacher asks.

No, we don't, you say, and you wonder why your son would do that?

Was it a desperate need for attention, a desire to perform, or is it some kind of defect, a compulsive need to lie, a condition that much of your father's family seems to have suffered from?

Jesus, is that genetic?

How do you ask your son why he did this? He will probably say nothing.

What did you do in school today?

Nothing.

No?

No, nothing.

You learned nothing?

Nothing.

What did you do during recess, lunch, art class, gym?

Nothing, nothing, nothing, and nothing. Nothing at all.

So you don't ask, not immediately. Why bother? Where will it get you?

Nowhere, that's where.

But when your son formally invites you to attend a parent-teacher conference in his bedroom that weekend, you go. You are happy to.

You walk into his room at the scheduled time and your son is sitting cross-legged in his baggy sweatpants in bed, shuffling papers, and so very serious that you sit when he asks you to.

When your son asks you if you know that your child lied in class, you say you heard something like that had happened, but that your son doesn't tell you much, and so you certainly don't know the whole story, not really.

Might the teacher be willing to share the story with you? you ask your son.

Of course, your son says.

Did you know that one of your son's friends had a dog that died? he says.

You do, you say. That's very sad, and it must be very hard for her.

It is, and did you know that your son stood up and said his dog died even though you don't have one because he thought his friend might feel better if she thought someone else had lost something they loved, but that it hadn't worked-out like he thought it would, that she didn't feel better, that he soon realized that he had made a mistake. Did you know that? your son says in a rush of words.

You did not, you say, but you think your son tried to do a wonderful thing, even if he was confused about how it might go. You also say that you are really proud of him, and ask that maybe the teacher could let him know this.

The teacher would be happy to share that with him, your son says.

Wonderful, you say, and maybe, because you know, our son doesn't tell us much, maybe, we could do this again some time? It's been very helpful.

Maybe we can, your son says, we will be sure to schedule something.

Which you hope he does, even if you have no idea how this came about and what it means about him, or you, or where any of this will go.

Loud

You consider it a betrayal, or at the very least, patricide, which may in fact be more horrific than the actual feeling you are trying to understand. But there is a feeling. It is strong and, yes, it sort of feels like death. You know that a son has to separate from his father, even defeat his father as necessary, if said son hopes to individuate. And you know this is true because it's all right there in *Oedipus Rex,* The Judgment, and *Finding Nemo.*

It is the morning of Thanksgiving and the two of you are visiting your family. You have an hour drive and you buy two new CDs for the trip, one by the punk band X and the other by kid folkster Dan Zanes.

You tell him you have a surprise and put in X.

Which should be good, but it is not.

No, he screams, that's not kids' music.

Sweetie, you say, it's X, you love X.

Which is true enough, though you are happy to acknowledge how much this makes you sound like the pseudo, hipster fathers you might otherwise want to make fun of in an attempt to cover-up your own pseudo, hipster fatherness.

No!

Okay, be cool, you say.

You put in Dan Zanes.

NO!

What, you say, you love Dan Zanes.

And he does, really, you are not making this up.

Dan Zanes is not kid music, he shouts

What are you missing here?

Hannah Montana is kids' music, he screams, and the Cheetah Girls, and *High School Musical*!

There it is.

His rejection of X may feel like a rejection of what makes you you, but it's not, not exactly.

It is his need to find his own way, separate from you and what you love.

Something you want to embrace, but you can't, not quite yet anyway.

And so tonight, while you are eating with him and the little one, and everyone is laughing, and getting loud, you think, one more try.

Do you want to get even louder? you ask.

Yeah, he says. How?

AC/DC, you say.

With "Highway to Hell" the walls begin to shake. With "Back in Black" the neighbors start milling around nervously in the hall. And by the time "Hells Bells" has saturated the building with its sheer awesomeness you have come to believe that a common ground has been forged with him, AC/DC somehow straddling the musical universe that exists between Kidz Bop and Be Your Own Pet.

He looks perplexed though.

What's wrong? you shout over the music.

You said you were going to play something loud, he says.

You realize then it doesn't matter what you do or how you do it. He is going to do what he is going to do, he is going to see the world as he sees it, and that's just how it's going to be.

His taste in music may suck, but he's trying to find his own way.

Run (Part I)

He will not come out.

He has stopped moving, pushing, gliding. He will not be born.

We have to remove him with forceps, the doctor says.

She is wearing a Minnesota Vikings sweatshirt, and you trust her, but you don't want this.

What? you ask, because what else is there to say?

What, what? We are going to do our best not to puncture his skull, she says matter-of-factly.

And that is that.

The doctor leans in and grabs his head with a pair of black salad tongs and this action is both amazingly gentle and fraught with violence all at once.

He comes out, beat-up like a prize-fighter, all bruise and muck.

Later, lying there on his mother's breast, with his tiny breaths, balled-up fists, and glowing skin, he is a ball of clay.

What he is at first is tears, always tears, and if not quite like his brother in terms of intensity, they are still there for a long time regardless.

He is longer to talk as well. And walk. He is longer to start these things anyway.

Yet he will sit there and smile, and he is like a donut, if you can imagine such a thing, and as you stare at this once little ball of clay, now donut, you wonder, because you have to, what he will be, and who he will become.

You must run and his older brother will not run, not then anyway, not at all. But this one, who knows? He is still unformed and the possibilities are endless.

Well, until he's not.

Because there he is on his feet, potty-trained, talking, explosive, and sudden, no panic, just go, and he will run, this one. You know he will run.

Which is good, because there is a race, a work thing, and the older one will not run, but this little one, he will, he is no longer a ball of clay, he is taking shape.

Do you want to run? you ask.

Okay, he says, just like that.

And then there he is toeing the line, so small and soft, his baggy sweat pants bunching up around his ankles, his number nearly the size of his shirt.

You try not to stare, but it's so hard, so you look away, but that doesn't work either.

So you look again.

He is adjusting the balloon bracelet on his wrist, the one that is shaped like a rocket ship.

You smile.

He suddenly bites his lower lip and tears begin to well-up in his eyes.

What, why, no?

It will be okay, you mouth to him, mentally imploring him just to run.

But he's not watching.

He is crying and he is staring off into space, and he is waiting, just as you are, and just as you have been for so long.

Then there is the gun, and he is running, and now you can't control yourself.

Not as you run along to meet him at the finish line.

Not as you scream for joy when he's done.

Not as you sob and gather him up in your arms as they place the finisher's medal around his neck, ever closer to the big world that awaits him.

Fingernails

You ask yourself if you were rushing, so focused on getting out of the house and away from parenting that you forgot how to be cautious. You wonder if you didn't want to leave it to the nanny. That, due to your guilt about watching someone else raise your son, you wanted to believe that you were useful too. What you know is that when you clipped his nearly indistinguishable fingernails you slipped. For a moment there was no sound, but, when that changed, the guilt that accompanied the subsequent cry was incomparably more traumatizing than that which preceded it. Worse things will happen to him. But you won't necessarily be the cause. And they won't hurt quite so much.

The Bear and the Skunk

Do not scream, yo. Do not, which is hard. Do not be physical either, yo, which is less hard. Still, he is making a scene, and action of some kind must be taken, and so you count to three and you focus on being patient.

How did you get here? What could you have done differently?

When does it end?

It started like it starts.

The little one does not want to read at bedtime with you, and that is fine, a little sad, but fine. He will not be reading with his mother tonight either. That is the deal. She is giving the older one some well deserved one-on-one time and this does not work for him.

It does not work at all.

You have told him that he is welcome to go to bed without reading, but that's no good either. What's also not good, from your perspective anyway, is crying in the hall.

So you are counting and when you hit three you steer him into his room for six minutes, one for each year he has been on this planet.

But that doesn't work for him either. Nor will him jumping up and down, but he's doing that anyway. It won't work, because being out of control can only lead to what it leads to, him somehow bumping his nose on the doorknob.

You want to be empathetic. You also want him to grow up. What you don't want to do is talk about his nose. You want him to calm down and you think that, if he can do so, then maybe you can too.

But he keeps talking about his nose.

Your nose still hurts, too bad, you finally say, trying to sound firm and in charge, though you really just sound like a dick.

You always say that, he says.

You do?

More tears, but then calm, and the two of you lying in bed, his beautiful sweaty face nuzzled into your neck.

You won't read, you say, there are consequences for that kind of behavior, but we can tell a story if you want, one sentence each, back and forth. Go.

There is a bear, he says, in an apartment.

And he is talking to a skunk, you say.

Right, but they're not talking, they're fighting, he says.

Okay, you say.

And then the bear bangs his nose on the doorknob, he says, and the skunk says, too bad. And that's sad.

It is, you say. The skunk was probably feeling very frustrated, you continue, but what could he have said instead that might have been better?

He could have said, are you okay, he says, that's the right way to do it.

It is, you say, it is, and then you say that you will try to do that yourself the next time something like this happens, because it will happen. It has to.

He smiles, and as he drifts off to sleep, you kiss him on the cheek, lingering there momentarily as you absorb the salty remains of his tears.

Anything But This

He is sitting on the couch, face forward, not smiling, and not looking at you. You are sitting at the dining room table, face forward, not smiling, and not looking at him.

The two of you are doing this per your suggestion.

You are both stuck in a moment, and how to get out of that moment just isn't clear, not while you're in it, and not while the agitation swirls around you like a cloud.

You are a writer and a social worker and you believe in the power of words and narrative to highlight the paths we may or may not take if just given the opportunity to see those paths more clearly.

He is a little boy and he could give a fuck about narrative, paths, or any of that.

He wants to watch television or play with his iTouch, maybe eat some cereal, anything really, anything but this.

Which is what again?

Oh yes, you are playing out a narrative of your making, reason enough for him not to give a fuck, because who cares about your fuckity-fuck narrative.

It went down like this, mostly, probably:

He didn't want to do his homework. Or, more accurately, he didn't want to correct his homework.

She doesn't care, he says, referring to his teacher, which may be true.

Only you care, he continues, which, along with your wife, may also be true.

So, should you not care so much? Because if not you, or your wife, then who?

Then again, does caring even matter?

Who knows?

But you do care. Or maybe more accurately, you care about him caring, and maybe that's because your parents didn't seem to care enough about your school work, or just didn't have to.

Maybe. Again, who knows? But is it also true that you can't care about this more than he does?

It is.

But does that stop you?

Sometimes, maybe, not so much.

So you push, possibly too much, and it goes something like this:

Slow down, please, you say. Take another look at that, check your work, something. C'mon, really.

No, I don't know it, he says, and I don't care.

You flinch.

At this point, you could ask yourself why this bothers you so much, not just the not caring, but his saying the actual words.

Because you don't know the answer to this, though you do know that words are important, that they convey a feeling, and that you suppose you don't want him to feel that way.

You could also ask yourself whether this is about his feelings or your feelings. How looking at him reminds you of you, the work you didn't do, the time you feel like you wasted.

Or you could just react.

Please use another phrase, you say, something that sounds more thoughtful and intelligent. It's not just your feelings about this that are upsetting, you continue, but the choice of language, too.

Okay, writer guy, he says. Are we done?

No, we're not, unless you're going to check your work, you say.

Why, no, why? he says. No one cares about this. Why is that so hard to understand?

There he goes again, you think. And what could be a more parental reaction than that?

This is a good time to breathe, walk away, and not pile even one more comment on top of the last, and the one before that, all of them piling up in a huge morass of frustration, his, yours, everyone's everywhere.

Apparently you are not built like that.

Then you must not care about watching television either, you say, that's cool.

Aaaaaah, he screams, coming at you, stopping, spinning, steaming, bouncing, freaking, all of it.

As you look at him, at yourself, this mess you're in, you think there must be another way. Maybe this calls for something different, because now you must be less like the parent you, and more like the work you, the you that doesn't get crazed and stupid and unable to think under duress.

Look, you say, let's lay out the narrative of how this is going to play out. You are spinning.

You are unhappy. We are unhappy. There will be more anger soon, and more unhappiness. It will not be good, and it will be followed by a time-out, for you, and then the loss of television, and who knows what else.

Yeah, he says with that fucking look that says he hates you and wants you to stop, though you won't, not now, because you are on a roll, and maybe, just maybe, a mission from God.

Or, you can sit down, you continue, we can sit down, at the couch, the table, not talking, just looking forward, getting calm, what have you. We can focus on breathing, the moment will pass, and peace will return. We could do that, right, yes we could, let's, good. Cool?

Nothing.

But now he is sitting on the couch, face forward and not looking at you, as you sit at the dining room table, face forward, and not looking at him, the agitation still swirling about the room.

And you call yourself a social worker, he suddenly mutters, low, and out of the corner of his mouth, just loud enough for you to hear.

Motherfucker, you think, shaking your head, yet smiling, laughing even, for the first time in a while. Since when?

Who knows? Not you certainly.

What you do know is that he will smile soon as well, eventually, possibly, definitely.

He will have to, because this moment won't last, it can't, not if you both breathe, get unstuck, and find a different path to travel on than the one you were heading down just moments ago.

I am Your Ancestor

When you were little he took you to the old Memorial Stadium to watch the Orioles play and always reminded you that few things were better, or more necessary, than drinking a cold beer at a baseball game. For years he did seven push-ups every morning and insisted that no man should wake-up and not pee first thing. It's how things are done. When you played cowboys and Indians with him he always suggested that the two sides make peace, something you never understood the utility of. All of that was a long time ago. He is slower now and walks stiffly, with a slight limp. The skin on his neck is loose and hard to shave, and the spare coarse whiskers sprouting here and there would have never made an appearance in the old days. He's skinny too, though his still handsome mug is easy enough to see, especially if you knew him when he was younger and fuller and quick with a laugh. He was, is, always curious, contrarian, vibrant, and full of questions, hitting every topic from every angle, and never letting you settle for answers that didn't, and don't, explore the political implications of the situation. Because there is always a political implication, be they overt like the Clinton impeachment trial, or less so like union bashing in the guise of cost savings. For him, it was never about how you felt about things or even what they looked like. It was about action and interaction, intimacy and physicality. You suppose this has changed little as his hearing has faded, his eyesight has begun to falter, and his heart, the biggest heart in the whole world, has started to fail him. And maybe all of that has something to do with his reaction to meeting your son, his great-grandson, for the first time, this lumpy ball of clay that can't discuss politics or deplore the state of the world, much less go to Orioles games or play handball as you did for years in the playgrounds of Baltimore. Or maybe it's something less complicated. He is old now, and he must wonder how much of himself he should share, and how much he ought to try when his time on earth is limited. Maybe not making any kind of personal connection is easier for everyone involved. So, despite how much he has to share, he is not sharing at all. Instead, he is cautiously circling your son and treating him as something fragile and foreign, and not able to engage, not now anyway. They look at each other, no interaction, no anything really, until with your mother's prompting, the old man approaches the small, hairy blob in front of him and puts up his hand for a high-five. Your son looks at him quizzically at first, and then warily, but then, smiling, he slaps hands with the old man, who smiles broadly as well, and says: I am your ancestor.

Unborn

He says to you, too bad it wasn't my dad, because that would be fine with me and better for the world as well.

He says this because he is a friend. He also says this because he hates his dad. But he especially says this because he doesn't know what it's like to lose a father. All he knows for sure is that your dad is dead now and not only will you never speak to him again, but he will never meet your unborn sons, something that seems just as cruel as dying too soon in the first place. You don't think your friend believes the world can possibly work like that. That the right people would die if we could somehow convince ourselves that the universe is fair and just. Of course, he doesn't consider the children who lost their fathers on September 11th and never got to experience half of what you did with yours. Nor does he know if he will ever speak to his father again. Whether they will someday reconcile and whether he will have children himself and be happy that his father is there to meet them. No, what he knows is his hatred and your profound sense of loss and confusion. What he also knows, or thinks he knows, is that this kind of thing should be more equitable. But it isn't, it can't be, and it certainly never will be. And this is the part that you can accept—that we have no control, that horrible things happen and that things we love can be torn from us with no true explanation. However, what you cannot accept is that your father will never meet those unborn boys, those boys he would love and who would love him back. The boys who would think he was so funny and charming, the grandpa who would have gotten on the ground with them to wrestle, who would have drawn with them and regaled them with epic stories of knights and dragons and unicorns that would somehow explode out of the vast recesses of his brain fully formed and complete. Your dad won't be there when they cry either, or when they perform on stage, something that might have led him to cry himself. Not that he cried when you were their age, not ever, but he was a dad then, and he thought he had to be tough. This would be different, though. He'd be softer. He'd have to be. Grandchildren strip away all that bullshit. That's just the way it is. The way it is not is how your friend wants it to be, and you tell him you're sorry it isn't that way, but not because you would wish a dead father on anyone, even someone who says he doesn't care, but because he wants to give you something to replace that something that is lost. But he can't, no one can. Those boys, those unborn boys will help, but the relationship with your father will not be replaced, because, sadly, it doesn't work like that either.

Is Anybody Out There?

You are lying there in bed, you and your wife, and you are as far apart as two people can be, even if the actual space between you is only inches.

The baby is sleeping in the Pack 'n' Play in your closet. He was in the room he shares with the older one, but that isn't working out tonight, so now he is in here with you, and the older one is in their room, the door shut, repeating the question—Is anybody out there?—over and over again.

As you lie there, you take a moment to disassociate, picturing yourself leaving your body and then the room itself, pausing to look at you and your wife before drifting through the window and away from all of this.

Arguably, it's easier to picture killing your wife, your children and yourself, rather than actually leaving them, which somehow seems much more destructive and impossible on the face of it.

You recognize that this is how things go wrong in those dark indie movies that Sundance loves. Someone makes a decision just like that. They choose murder over merely opening a door and walking away forever because in getting caught up in the throes of something they can't figure out, it just seems easier.

But this isn't Sundance and you know that you definitely aren't killing anyone or going anywhere, and that you and your wife are in this together until the end, bloody or otherwise.

At this point, the two of you are still miles apart and staring at the ceiling, searching for escape hatches and trying to ignore the calm but persistent question emanating from the next room: Is anybody out there?

Hey, you say, not looking at her. This isn't going to be any *Kramer vs. Kramer* thing. If someone leaves, and I'm not saying I want that, but if someone leaves, they don't get to leave the kids behind, so that the parent who stays has to learn how to make French toast and possibly bang some hot young associate from work. Well, I guess the banging part would be fine, but the rest of it, no, can't have it. Deal?

Something shifts here, as you hoped it would. The chasm between the two of you has shortened.

You roll towards each other and just stare for a moment. It's amazing how much the boys look like her and how lucky that makes them because she's so fucking beautiful and always has been.

Deal, she says smiling.

And, with that, you smile too.

Salpicon

—for Noah

You turn your back to him, and jam your hands into your pockets. It is raining and your every thought is dark, infused with anger and ready to take flight. You stare off into the distance and you do not look at him. Yet, you can picture him crouching there, not moving and watching you. He is bemused, lips pursed, smirking. You think about his beautiful skin and the missing tooth that somehow enhances his smile. The baby fat is all burned away now, but you can still clearly remember his birth, the forceps, the black eyes, the fear and excitement. You can't remember why you were so angry with him just moments ago. Why you gripped his skinny little arms the way you did before turning away. Is this about your own unrealized hopes and dreams, the loss of freedom that parenting brings or is it your endless inability to express pain and confusion? Because how could it be about him? He is so small with everything yet to come. But you cannot make sense of it, and so you don't even attempt to look at him until he walks over, hugs your legs and whispers, sorry.

Moving

He's just walking down the street in front of you. It's what they do of course, walk and breathe, and all those things people engage in when they're alive and they're growing.

He's in front of you and he's not holding your hand or looking at you, and that's different, new. You're not even on his radar.

Did you see when she kicked him at recess? your older son says to his friend all mock serious.

Yeah, she replies, he got treated.

Treated, your son says laughing, that's not how you use the word treated.

No, she says, what's treated?

It's like when you say, your mom is so fat that when she stands in front of the sun it's like a total eclipse. That's getting treated, he says.

And they both laugh.

His enormous backpack is swaying to and fro. His lunch bag hanging there off a hook, the lunch he made, wrapped and packed himself.

At the moment though, he's just walking along, talking, joking and so far away from you.

He never was soft, not like the little one, who is walking along beside you and holding your hand.

But this is something new, different. He has muscles now and what he claims is the start of pubic hair, though he called it penis hair when he told you about it the night before, after his shower.

Look, he said, there's like ten of them. Look, right there.

You looked. You didn't want to, but you did. You didn't see much, but you smiled anyway and said good work.

Good work?

You watch him some more, and you try to figure out what this moment means, because it means something, right? It must.

Though maybe that's a parent thing, the need to add meaning to stuff that is otherwise normal, regular, expected. Things that are what they are, nothing more or less, just what is.

Still, isn't this the same kid who wouldn't leave your side at school drop-off just this time last year? Who until recently ran into traffic rather than encounter a dog? Who wouldn't leave the house if it was windy?

It is, and yet there he was, what, last weekend, running in the park with three dogs, big dogs, all of them being buffeted by the wind, and all of them full of frolic and joy.

So what does all this mean? You want it to mean something. It has to. Every moment does now.

He gets farther ahead, still laughing and talking and fighting and walking that big kid walk, and you know what it means. It means he is moving away from you, venturing on, and he has to. This is how it works, and you have to encourage it, and you will.

But it's real now, really real, and once there is movement, there is movement away, and it must be celebrated, even as you hold on to it, and even as you begin to chase after him.

You know this moving away from you is something you always said you wanted, but you still cannot bear the idea of actually witnessing it, not yet anyway.

Run (Part II)

Can we get ice cream? the little one says.

We can get ice cream, yes, of course, you say.

Can we get Sponge Bob? he says.

It is hot and Sponge Bob is big and messy, with his drippy bubble gum eyes, and no, you don't want him to have Sponge Bob.

But he has all the power.

You are supposed to have the power, but you don't.

He has it because you want to run. His mom and brother are not home. And so he goes with you or you do not go.

Sponge Bob is fine, you say.

You pack extra wipes and paper towels, another T-shirt, and jam him into the baby jogger.

Faster, he says when you hit the sidewalk.

Can't, you say, trying to find some rhythm, pushing you.

You're old, he says, and slow.

Maybe, you say, but still handsome. Don't forget that.

Still, he isn't wrong. You are slow, and more so every day, and every year, and maybe now that he's gotten older, and you can run more often, and more easily, your slowing has slowed, but that doesn't make you fast, not by a long shot. You are old and out of shape. Your knees hurt most of the time. As does your back and even your shoulders.

So yes, you are slow.

But you are still holding on to the idea of running, regardless.

You have to.

Why do you have to, though, and might you be doing something else that brings this same feeling?

You wonder.

Running is freedom and liberation, an escape from doubt, fear, and confusion, and this holds true even when you're out pushing him.

And what could replace that?

Nothing you've found yet, not quite, not even writing, not exactly. How long can you keep this up?

Where's the ice cream man? he asks.

We have to get out to the lake first, you say, breathless, already feeling the sweat pooling on your lower back, behind your knees, and just above your brow.

When do we get to run together? he asks.

What, he wants to run? Where? How? Together, really? Because that is something worth holding on for.

You try not to get too excited. You try to breathe.

What do you mean? you say. Like, how old do you have to be?

No, like today, he says. Can we run today?

You look down, the sweat sliding along your wrists. He is so small, and competing in an organized kids' dash as he has done is one thing, but could this work? No, how?

Then again, why couldn't it?

Right now, you say, expecting that to be that.

Yes, stop please, he says.

You stop.

He pops out of the baby jogger and stands next to you, no taller than your hip.

Let's go, he says.

And so you go along the sidewalk, across the street, into the park, under the highway.

Stride for stride.

Little arms pumping.

Breathing slowly.

People staring, everyone. It's so weird-looking, but he is so smooth, and you are so proud, though self-conscious too, wondering if people think you have forced him to do this.

You are now well into the park and you have run at least half a mile, though maybe more, and then he stops, just like that.

Done, he says.

Okay, you say.

And yes, this you can hold on to: running together, really running together. That is something.

Stay cool, you think.

Don't get too excited and talk about it, what it means, your plans for the future, all that. And don't think about how you used to run with your dad either, no tears, not tears of joy, or sadness. Keep it cool, keep it cool, keep it cool.

But you can't, not totally anyway.

Hey, we should do this again, you say, and maybe even race together some day too.

Do you see the ice cream man, he says?

Not yet, you say, but be patient. He will come, and it will happen.

And it will come, and it will happen. Soon, you think, all of it.

Puzzles

You are running late, always running late to pick up the older one at daycare, and it is five dollars for every minute past 6:00 p.m., which is already late enough as it is, but there you are again, trying to do one last thing in the office, missing a train, sitting on a train, stopping to buy the kid a snack at the scary bodega on Division, and running through the rain to prevent being late. You are so close, the watch reading 5:55, then 5:56, suddenly 5:58, but you are at the door now, buzzing and bursting in, where it's so quiet that it's not clear to you whether any children are still there at all.

Then you see them, a group of kids and the teacher, the young guy, all of them fresh-faced and sweaty, sitting in a big group, leaning forward and intently looking at something. You slow down, you try to catch your breath and you tell yourself that it's okay. You made it on time and everything will be okay. You walk up to see what everyone is looking at.

It is your kid.

He's in the middle of thousands of puzzle pieces, and he is methodically putting together the biggest puzzle you've ever seen in your life. Everyone is transfixed, as are you, it's beautiful, like a ballet, and you watch and you think about a story you must have read in *The New York Times* about how our biggest fears are the most irrational.

Like flying in a plane is immensely safer than getting in your car, but flying has a hold on our collective fears that a car will never match.

And this is how parenting has been from the start.

You never worry about how you will pay for his college, which on purely technical level is mostly impossible to do at this time, but you endlessly worry about things like Leukemia, porch parties gone awry, and every possible accident that could lead to irreparable brain damage.

It is all there, all of it, and all of the time, which is not even to mention your ongoing fear about the boys being sexually abused because you somehow turned away at the wrong time.

You also never worry about whether your kid is special, or if he has some kind of gift. You've come to assume it, though based on what, or how, you don't know.

On the other hand, maybe this puzzle thing means something. It must, but, again, you don't really know.

Just like you don't know exactly why a fresh-faced young man chooses to work around small children—something you know is antiquated and fucked-up—so you push it aside, and take a moment and enjoy what's happening before you: your beautiful genius boy doing something bizarre and awesome to the amazement of all who are watching.

Answers

He knows.

It doesn't matter that he's little and doesn't seem to know anything. He knows she's different, that her family is different, different than us certainly, and just different, period.

She is the queen of the playground, with her long hair blowing in the wind and her flip-flops thrown among the detritus as she walks barefoot along the top of the monkey bars.

He is mesmerized, you are mesmerized. She is a vision, and she is nothing like him. She is fearless and free to be whatever it is she wants to be.

You wonder if her awesomeness has something to do with the fact that she has two dads, but you don't know. You don't even know what you don't know.

What you do know is that the dad who doesn't stay at home tends to be in the playground at night, like you, when the work day is over. And that he smiles a lot.

What you also know is that your kid thinks he knows something about some part of this, and he wants, even needs, answers about all of it.

So? he asks.

Excuse me, he says to the dad. Where's her mom?

There is no mom, smiling dad says to him, nicely, if maybe a little bluntly.

Your kid is being friendly, though how he knows she has two dads, as opposed to a mom and a dad, isn't so clear to you. Apparently they know things even when you can't imagine that they do.

There's a mom, your kid says, there's always a mom.

And of course there is.

No, the dad says, no mom here, maybe you're thinking of the nanny?

He's still friendly, still smiling, but he's not budging either. You've never seen a mom yourself, but you have wondered about this as well.

There are younger siblings and they all look like alike enough that there must be some kind of arrangement. Not that you would ever ask.

But your kid will.

I know what a nanny is, your kid says, I have one, and I've seen yours. But the mom, what's up with the mom?

I have to go, smiling dad says, walking away.

He could have been more helpful. Aren't there a million things he could have said while still protecting his privacy?

He may not want to be gay dad spokesman, and he may be worried that your kid might say something to his daughter that he doesn't want her to know yet, and all that's fine you suppose, but now you must decide what you will say, because your kid is going to have questions, and questions require answers.

She does have two dads, right? your kid asks you?

She does, you say, hoping you can leave it at that, because how much detail can you go into about same sex relationships with someone so little? What's too much? And how do you ever know?

Are they married, he says staring at you intently with those endlessly brown eyes of his. Can boys get married?

You wonder now if it's not the mom that he's interested in learning more about. Maybe it was always about having two dads and trying to figure that out.

It also might be that you're just doing what parents do, filtering your kid's question through what you wish you knew about him.

But sometimes a question is just a question, right?

You decide to be as straightforward as the smiling dad was not.

Boys can only get legally married in Massachusetts you say, but they can be in love anywhere, that's the important thing, sometimes boys love boys and girls love girls, and that's cool.

No reaction, nothing.

Do you have any questions about that? you ask.

No.

And that's that, until it isn't.

A year later, there's a baby, a little brother, and he, the big one, says to you that he plans to marry his mother.

The advice in the parenting books is that the correct response to this assertion is no, your mommy is already married to someone and you will need to marry someone else.

Which is what you say, to which he replies, fine, I will marry him then, the baby, and while it seems impossible that this tiny, near feral creature will ever marry anyone, you still feel the need to respond to this, to somehow control the situation more than may be required.

You can't marry your brother, you say.

To which he replies, but you said boys can get married in Massachusetts.

And he has you there.

Caught Off Guard

There is a flash of red hair like fire, or cinnamon, and it shakes you out of the world you were completely lost in.

You are writing. Well, you were writing.

It is Sunday morning, the children are asleep, and so this is when it must be done.

It is peaceful, the sunlight forcing its way through the cracks in the blinds, the dust jumping from sunbeam to sunbeam, the occasional car on the street below, or the flush of a toilet somewhere in the building, every sound permeating the otherwise quiet room.

Still, it has to end, it always does. Someone has to wake-up. Lately it has been the little one, the one who sleeps in long T-shirts and tiny briefs, the Angry Birds displayed across his behind. He is like a donut, his caramel skin so soft to the touch, and you want to consume him, always, and endlessly.

He drifts out into the living room like a small wave, and, as he arrives, one part of the day ends, and another begins.

Today is different though.

He is wearing pajama bottoms, soft, flannel, some kind of blue and white geometric pattern too complicated to decipher this early in the morning.

And he is wearing pajama bottoms because he is not alone.

She is here, his best friend, and she is trailing behind him, her long red hair catching the morning sun and bursting into flame right before your eyes.

They do not see you.

They are lost in their own world.

Should we watch Pokemon? she says, brushing the hair out of her face as she plops down on the couch in her long pink V-Neck shirt.

Yes, he says, smiling that smile that reminds you of your grandmother. Would you like some cereal?

He is so polite, so caring. Who is this little boy, and what has he done with your baby son?

Even as you lose yourself in their conversation, the image of them leaving his room together sticks with you, unwilling to budge or drift away.

This is different, isn't it, girls sleeping over with boys? When did that start and why is everyone so cool with it?

Not that you aren't cool with it, and not that your parents ever had to worry about such a thing. You didn't even talk to girls until middle school. It was all too scary, weird, and impossible.

But he lives in a different world, one where this happens, and, as you lose yourself in this, you can't help but picture him in college, and later the real world, drifting from his room with a girl in tow, older and independent, in love, or something, and building a life, his own life, and how is that possible?

It isn't, not really, it can't be.

You stare at them sitting on the couch, smiling at each other, manipulating the remote, so content with this life they have.

You could stare at them forever, but he catches you looking and he looks back, bemused, and caught off guard.

You wonder what comes next, but you don't have to wait long to find out.

Will you get us cereal? he asks. We're already sitting.

And with that the day truly begins.

Socks

He is on the floor, the younger one. He is crying and kicking his legs. He looks like a dying cockroach. Not that you tell him this. He doesn't like cockroaches, and he definitely doesn't like any reference to dying.

Instead you focus on the task at hand: Kid on the ground, crying and flailing.

Why might that be?

Did the older one punch him? It doesn't look like it, the older one is nowhere to be seen.

Is it windy? Not so much, and not inside your apartment certainly.

Did a dog walk by? Seems unlikely, you don't own a dog.

But then you take another look at him and you know exactly what it is.

It's the fucking socks.

Again.

They are not straight enough, he says.

Let me help you, you say.

There is too much material hanging off of the heel, he says.

We'll fix it, you say.

You can't fix it, he says.

You want to ignore him. It might even be better parenting to do so.

But you can't. School is starting.

The new pair rubs my ankle the wrong way, he says.

But that's only a problem when they are right side out, but not so much when they are inside out, right? you say, somewhat desperately, not sure what will work, and trying to ignore the older one, whose socks are fine and just wants to leave now.

What? the younger one says.

They feel better when they are inside out, right? you repeat. Your eyes are burning.

What does that mean? he screams, tears and mucous flying everywhere.

He's so loud. He wants to be quiet and more relaxed, you think, but he can't be. He has no idea how that works yet.

And so there are more tears, endless tears, and frustration, his and yours, because why don't the socks work? Didn't they work yesterday?

Yes, maybe they did, eventually.

You have to force yourself to remember, in these moments, as his face turns red and ugly, swollen with pain and confusion, that he's just a little boy, the socks just don't work, and it's not that he wants to be upset, much less upset you. It's not purposeful, or calculated, it's that he wants them to somehow work better and he has no idea how to make it so.

You turn the socks inside out and help him slip them on, and then his shoes.

No, these don't fit inside my shoes, and they are not my socks, they are his socks, he says pointing to his brother. Why don't you know that.

We will work it out, you say. We can get another pair of socks.

You run down the hall to get more socks and you think this pair, this pair will work, maybe, and maybe someday the socks will always work. They will make sense.

He won't be a little boy anymore, but someone else.

Someone bigger and older, and who may struggle with work, relationships, dashed dreams, his own children, and a million other things, though hopefully not too many or too much, because you cannot bear the thought of him struggling any more than is necessary.

Still, even as you run down the hall, and even as you know that you cannot control any of that, you also know that you can mostly count on the fact that he may face many problems, but his socks probably won't be one of them.

He will have gotten passed it, because that's just how it works.

The Princess

Part One: Snow White

BL Pawelek

For my daughter, Abbey Road

Some day when spring is here
We'll find our love anew
And the birds will sing
And wedding bells will ring
Some day when my dreams come true

—Someday My Prince Will Come

seven circles surround you

they have come
from straight winds
jumping straight rays
from the sun to slide the lands

the birds will look for you
animals hiding you away
in deep woods
away from sound and song

seven circles surround you
surround and protect the lights
protect the shadows

they guide you though
sleep dreams of lambs
i count the sun
work along the shadows
just out of sound and sight

there are people
that miss your name
miss writing the letters
on cold walls

lullaby

when your eyes will not close
you throw pillows at faeries
and their shadows

the feathers don't drop
brush color on your cheeks
while the red one reads
of other happily ever afters
and lost dreams
found with kisses

you shake
colored sheep running
through stars never caught
but close your eyes
with a deep breath
and slowly let it go

break skin

walk through the doors
one through another
aging each growing
and containing
stretching flesh strong with
a piece of my heart
on your back

run the grass wild turkeys
and feathers floating on sun
the birds sing and sing
and continue

the long years of winter
and cold growth
waiting for the daughter
to break skin

sugar and rows

your words
beautiful and foreign
and nine minutes of life
a slow drum beat
carrying me to the tower top in sunlight

children's voices singing
testament bible songs
i hesitate the first empty step
waving in wind
but when the foot leaves the steel
you push

the cousin from far

she throws her hands
tries to fly away
from other sisters ugly and fight
the stars do not light
the blue sky

she looks for the prayer
with one good idea
a neck that fits
one good hand
or four

the mad one ties it down
never letting the hope
the happiness the dance
of french women and windows

dancing with eyes closed

the red bows in wood boxes
clean and soft with apples
you run your hands
through the cloth and dream
of tomorrow past horizon

the tiny men inside
smashing their plates
and losing their day plans
accidents in the wood clearing

rain will come
animals will scatter
only for a count of five
then the sun and prince
dry food and dry clothes

musical instruments
and animal sounds
and wondering

the kiss is coming from the woods

stars drop on us
to sleep for years
until kisses run the landscape

the wall knights
grey beards and black iron
against windows with kings asleep

the monsters will line
up against us claws and horns
foxes calling in the dark
the moon hiding away

remember the youth
running and flowers
rings glowing on fingers
of red paint and dresses
the kiss is coming
from the woods

The Princess

Part Two: Aurora

BL Pawelek

For my daughter, Abbey Road

"I know it's true that visions
are seldom all they seem
But if I know you, I know
what you'll do
You'll love me at once"

—Once Upon a Dream

running the castle

they float
the faeries of geometry
circle triangle and square
with their small sticks
waving

the blue one merriweather
runs her hand through my hair
and whispers

when you slept
cardinals and canaries
flew your soft bed
i ran piano notes
over your dreams

we felt the fire
from the far hills
the oak wheel spinning
heating the spring nights
through march

in my dreams
i saw you sleeping
under purple sheets
the candles always burning

the minute no longer

pink girls ride
along the blue half circle
running and glide
the heart shaped purple turf
we will all become the future

the minute no longer
counted down
only parts of you will age
the non memory
and action of legs

the wind blows
through hot mess
to small smiles
blue eyes and youth
guarding and aware

the sun turns around your neck
sets along the curls of hair

the green one

circle clouds
around the mountains
and the growls of all animals
the paths higher
turns and raising until drop

the black birds keep their eyes
circle the castle and forbidden

we have seen her once
and stood strong as she swept
through the shadows
through the last minutes
of metal pointing to the skies

water dreams on dry land

we rest on the flat of lakes
wrap the two suns
from morning and wait the wind

the loons call
from the long distance
ask you to become once more

your hand on the side of the boat
squeezing and blood

after we sprint
down the docks and jump
you breathing air and then water

battle lake does not fight you
it holds and loves
and you stay with me
along the peninsula
and back to the woods
back to the shade and paths
to your water dreams on dry land

invest in propers

you rest your head
on orange
that is inside cool
of the blue
i try to untie
try to think of tomorrows
invest in propers

we will leave
this sunshine land
stop in zone of lakes
and friendly and slow

we will light everything
crush the dirt
drag the beautiful across
a grounded thousand miles
to place back in the sky

sleep with wolves and lambs

colored leaves roll the wind
change orange and brown
capturing sun
and the softness of grass

you cover yourself
the blanket of all lengths
sleep with wolves and lambs

the october sun still warm
along the white lines white bars
the test and hold of all things

in your rest hands
the dreams of all girls
the last winds circling
the deep sleep and breath

crash the silos

the brown wisps in blue sky
love of all things
i will live in you
forever

you will break the harvest
with tools of hands
you will know your name
when the music plays
ever after and again

you will crash the silos
hands holding water
as you push to the sun
hear the words and letters
hear the prayers of yesterday

allow the moon

the sunshine hair
glow and curl and sandy dogs
delicate enough to feed
butterflies the sugar sand

her princesses raise the morning
cover the night allow the moon
her prince makes dreams come true

the thorns dragons and dark mountains
eclipse away await the departure
shining clear the sun shows all
the asleep now awaken
the dead hearted

now with a touch of red
the crown with all jewels shining

the prince does exist

the trees will grow
straight for you
every leaf perfect and green
every branch without thorn

the grey of dirt
will brush off your dresses
fall to the wind
and be carried to the oceans

the green light
at the top of the stairs
does not exist
there are no fingers and wheels
no sleep to be afraid of

the prince does exist
a hand for your slender
a lead step during the dance
during the dream

Everything is Getting Worse

Dave Housley

For Lori and Ben

Burns wakes up knowing something is wrong. It is quiet. Too quiet. It is never quiet like this, not anymore. He sits up, listens. No Rachel jabbering on the phone with her mother, no *Real Housewives* shouting from the television, no treacly Justin Bieber crap bouncing out from Tyler's room.

Justin Bieber. Jesus Christ. Even the name is ridiculous. Awkward and a little gay. Angus Young. That's a name. A rock star name. Ozzy Osbourne. David Lee Roth. You can practically see the balls on a name like that. They might as well have been named Sperm Balls. Or Fucking Machine. Weird, he thinks, that there was never a band named Fucking Machine. Or anything with sperm in it. But Justin Bieber? Everything about it is wrong. Soft. What kind of name is Bieber anyway? German? Is it made up? But who would make up a name like that? What kind of rock star doesn't have a made up name anyway? Everything is different now. Worse.

It is too early to even think about the kid's hair.

How many days until that concert? He checks his phone. Three days. He will have to come up with tickets and accompany Tyler to this concert—drive down Connecticut Avenue into the city, fight the traffic, pay for parking, pray that they don't see anybody from the basketball league or any of his male clients, deal with the fact that they are in the one percentile of males at the concert of a pubescent boy, then actually sit through the music, which, holy shit, he hadn't even considered the actual concert itself before. The alternative is to watch his son mope around, lock himself in his room, cry his little boy tears over the fact that his father has not been able to produce the one thing this entire year that the boy has actually asked for, has been asking for since Christmas and then his birthday two months later. The boy, so confident that his father will in fact produce that he has stopped asking, has circled the date on his Justin Bieber calendar, has consulted with Rachel numerous times over the past week about the availability of his chosen outfit for this event. Every time Burns tells the boy it is not such a sure thing, that the concert, for instance, has been sold out for months, Tyler just smiles as if Burns is telling a favorite old joke. If he wasn't such a good kid, this would be an easy call—no tickets, tough break, kid, maybe next time. But every time he thinks about the kid's faith in him, Burns nearly breaks into tears.

He is screwed either way.

He sits up. Where the hell are they? Maybe her water broke? No, she would wake him for that, would wake him for anything eight months in. Last week she woke him to retrieve a glass from the cupboard. The week before, to go get the newspaper, her and able-bodied, nine-year-old Tyler curled up with the *Real Housewives* while Burns limped out to the sidewalk in his boxers.

He rolls out of bed and walks to the bathroom. The Achilles are hurting a little worse than yesterday. The bursitis in his elbow is throbbing. From what? Raking the leaves? He pauses. What did he do yesterday? It must be from raking the leaves. Jesus, getting old is fucking terrible, and he's only forty three. It's going to be downhill from here. He limps to the bathroom. Anything would be better than this slow decline, like an old computer that steadily becomes obsolete, larded with obscure files that nobody will ever use again, cookies, spam, out of date programs, a faulty and comically reduced memory, until finally the machine itself is a joke, a novelty, a disposal problem.

He looks to the medicine cabinet. Today will be the day he will stop. Cold turkey. One day at a time. He is not the kind of person who gets into situations like this. He can picture them in there, the friendly peach color that says this is not anything terribly serious. He can feel the burn in his throat, the twitch in his nose, the feeling like shotgunning coffee and all of sudden everything seems not so bad. Do-able.

But no. Not today. This kind of thing is for the weak, for fifteen year old girls and latchkey trailer park kids, not forty-three year old pharmaceutical sales representatives.

"Hey buddy!" Burns jumps. Not again. It is the voice of Ryan Seacrest, happy and peppy and vacant. For the past six months, ever since the Adderall, he's been hearing Ryan Seacrest in his head. If the company hadn't scaled their medical coverage back two years ago and were still paying for psychiatry, Burns might have even sought help. As it is, he tries to put it out of his mind. Thinking too much about what all this means would not be good.

"A little early for the old A powder isn't it?" Seacrest says.

"Fuck you," Burns groans. "I'm not crazy."

"Right-ee-o," Seacrest says. For some reason, Seacrest talks, always, like a fifties radio deejay. "But still. Justin Bieber. Bieber Fever. The United States of Bieber, right?"

"Right?" Burns says.

"Just saying," Seacrest says, "that's gonna be a tough one. Get through that without any of the old Burnsy's little helper."

Sometimes it works to just ignore it, go about his business. He sits on the toilet, waits, picks up a magazine, *Clean Living*, picks up another, *Prevention*. He remembers when Rachel's magazines were *Cosmopolitan* and *Glamour*. Things have changed. The woman on the cover of *Prevention* is pretty hot, though, in a grown-up woman kind of way. She is probably the same age as Rachel, and look at her with the flat belly and the perky tits. Eyes that don't look like a goddam *Doonesbury* character. He regards his own midsection. He has no room to talk. Sinking. Everything is sinking. He pages into *Prevention*—even the name is a defeat, a recognition that there's something, a million things to be prevented, avoided, blocked with lunges and superfoods and envisioning success, with bedroom secrets and six small meals a day, slimming colors and power moisturizers and belly-buster yoga poses and closet organization secrets. He flips the pages, searching for more pictures of the woman on the cover. She looks a little like

Tyler's friend's mother. The lawyer. Divorced. The one he imagines is always on her way to a fabulous dinner party where good looking, accomplished people sit around the table and say witty things, a scene from one of those romantic comedies that Rachel insists on watching when they have a rare "date night."

Date night. Date night used to be a garter belt and a blowjob. Now it's more like a Jennifer Aniston movie and carry out from the Italian place.

Maybe just a quick hit from the medicine cabinet? He can feel it, the initial rush, then the buzz, then his senses tightening and focusing and also somehow loosening up. It is the only thing that gets him through another terrible day of calling on doctors who no longer have time for him, through the small concessions and defeats, the steady retreat that makes up his day. The bottle is right there in the medicine cabinet. It would be easy. Maybe just one more day.

Plenty of people do it and they are, what, graduating from Harvard, becoming the next generation, getting a goddam trophy for going to French class or starting social marketing internet companies.

No, he thinks. He has a wife, a son, another one on the way. It's time to get his shit together. Should be easy to stop. If he wants to.

He pages into *Prevention,* finds the article. There's another picture of the cover lady. This time she's in profile, in running clothes. Nice ass, too. Damn. He reads the headline: "Edible Eating: Food Cures for Cancer." What ever happened to *Cosmopolitan*? Those articles were all about oral sex and how to look hotter. *Cosmo* was more like *Playboy* than it wasn't. And now this. Everything is getting worse all the time.

Another reason to hit up the medicine cabinet. But Adderall? He could have gotten himself addicted to a grown up drug. Heroin, cocaine, booze.

At least he'd be in good company. Keith Richards, John Belushi, any number of badass rockers and writers and artists have been addicts and drunks.

The front door opens and he hears the familiar rustle of Rachel and Tyler. Tyler clomps down the hall. Rachel puts away groceries—more clean living, no doubt—flax seed oil and kale and organic macaroni and cheese. What's the point of organic macaroni and cheese, anyway? It's supposed to be bright orange and made of who knows what. Every person Burns knows was raised on shitty macaroni and cheese, loves it to this day, and it's not because the Kraft company bought local and stayed away from chemicals.

He again tries to remember if Rachel got like this when she was pregnant with Tyler. Maybe it is just a phase, one that will pass like the swollen breasts and morning sickness. All he can remember from the first few months after Tyler's birth is a hazy, sleep-deprived feeling of desperation, an instant nostalgia for a time he had only just a few months ago passed through, and the terror that, even though things weren't really that great before the baby, nothing would ever be so easy again.

And then it starts up. Bieber. He wonders at the lightness of it all. It is like they put every terrible pop song from the past twenty years into a grinder and pressed the results straight onto a CD. Not even a CD anymore. Onto a file. A cloud.

He used to joke with Leon that they were going to lock the boy in his room with nothing but a guitar and the first four Van Halen records, let him out when he was eighteen. That is seeming like a better idea every day.

Nothing is happening in his bowels. He stands. Goddam the elbow hurts. Raking the leaves? Jesus. He opens the medicine cabinet and then closes it. His gut is tightening, turning. Soon, he knows, he will be a little sick.

"Baby bay-by bay-by oooooh," Bieber sings. Tyler—his own son—is singing along. The boy is only nine and he seems more interested in this music than in basketball, or football, or playing in the mud, or riding his bicycle, or any of the things Burns sees the other neighborhood boys doing every day. Tyler just wants to stay in his room, singing and dancing along to these sunny, overproduced, soulless pop songs. The first time Burns heard Bieber, he thought it was Rihanna or Taylor Swift, Lady Whatshername, one of the usual pop tweens dandied up and trotted out by whatever corporation owns all the other ones now. He can't keep track of any of this shit anymore.

And if he can actually get tickets to this concert? What the hell is that going to be like? This pop drivel for what, an hour and a half of dancing and choreography, a light show and fifty thousand screaming tween girls? It would be too much to bear.

But Tyler is so innocent, so sure that his father will provide for him, and how many more years do they have of that?

He puts on sweatpants and a t-shirt and carries his high-tops down the hall toward Tyler's room. "Baby bay-by bay-by," Bieber sings. The sound must be turned up to ten, but it is always turned up to ten now. They lost that argument long ago. Now, with the baby due any day, Rachel has checked out to the extent that Burns wonders if she even realizes she's still sharing the house with two males. If you hypnotized her, he thinks, there is a fair chance she would tell you she is living in one of the cities with the Real Housewives. He is curious which one she would pick, but he can't tell the difference between them well enough to even venture a guess.

He hears them now, as he walks down the hall, bickering and shouting at one another over the tinkle of wine glasses. "Ohmygawd," Rachel groans.

"You okay?" he shouts. He knows she is but this is as close as he can get to making a point lately.

"Ne-ne is such a bitch," she says. "It's pretty awesome."

He knocks on Tyler's door. "Hey buddy," he says. Keyboards. Electric drums. Bieber sings "I thought you'd always be mine..."

He knocks again, opens the door a crack.

"Daaaaaaaaad!" Tyler shouts. His voice is high and smooth. A tenor. Not unlike Bieber. If only he could find the boy somebody else with whom he shares something—some thin, scrappy point guard, perhaps. Or a shortstop. One of those kids from the vampire movie. Anything would be better than this.

"Hey buddy," Burns says. "You wanna go over to the park, shoot some hoops?"

The boy pauses. God bless him, Burns thinks. He still wants to please his Dad. He wants to want to go play basketball.

"Or maybe go for a hike? We could go out to the lake or something."

Tyler looks to his dresser. "It's just," he says, "we got the new DVD. Mom said I could watch it this afternoon. You know the concert is only a few days?" With this last phrase, his voice goes up even more, a question and a confirmation, all at once.

Burns sighs. Tyler has his eyes—blue and complicated—and behind them, Burns can see wheels turning. "I told you. I'm not even sure we can get tickets to that concert. It's been sold out for a long time. I have a lot of work right now." He gestures to the living room. "Plus, your mother. I mean, it's not a great time right now for something like the, um. The Bieber."

Tyler laughs. He punches Burns in the arm. "Dad," he says, with real affection. The lump forms quickly in Burns' throat. His eyes tear. What is happening to him lately? He practically broke down watching *SportsCenter* last night. Is this some kind of male menopause?

"Okay," he says, hoping the boy can't hear the emotion in his voice. "We'll do the park some other time." He ruffles Tyler's hair, a habit he thought had gone out of style with the *Andy Griffith Show* until he found himself doing it constantly, a fatherly show of affection that seems loving but somehow manly. Old school. The boy is smart enough, aware enough to understand that he is, in some way, letting his father down. Burns does not want to be that kind of father —the one who earns respect but not love. The kid is a good kid. Sweet. If he has terrible taste in music, if he is a little obsessed with the latest pop sensation—if he does, in fact, have Bieber Fever—then the best Burns can do is wait it out and let the kid follow his own nine-year-old heart. He closes the door, walks toward the kitchen.

Bieber sings "bay-be bay-by bay-by..."

It's so light and stupid. And that hair. Tyler is trying to grow his hair into some reasonable approximation of Bieber's own helmet head, a cut that Burns associates most strongly with female figure skaters from the seventies.

But that was thirty-some years ago, when Burns himself was Tyler's age. The boy has no idea that his idol has a girl's haircut, a girl's voice, and a following that is mainly a bunch of girls. The kid just knows what he likes. And whose job is it to expose him to new things, to lead the boy? His father's, of course.

And like that, Burns knows what he has to do.

He walks into the living room, where Rachel is reclining on the sofa, her belly pushing ahead of her, swollen and ready to pop. On the television, a group of women in cocktail dresses are gathered in a semi-circle around a smirking host. One of the women stands, throws her chair to the ground, stomps away from the camera.

"Ohmygod," Rachel says. As usual, her voice sounds removed, as if she was underwater.

Burns knows she is talking to him and not talking to him. "I'm taking Tyler to that Bon Jovi concert tonight," he says.

"Deena is completely crazy," she says. "Oh. My. God."

"Well," Rachel asks. "How was your little experiment?"

Burns throws his shirt into the closet. It is late. That is just one of the things he hadn't really thought about. In theory, it was a fantastic idea – the only thing to do.

"Well?" Rachel says. For once, the television is off. She is reading a magazine about celebrity haircuts, the pages interestingly marked with sticky notes. Burns wonders what she could possibly be planning.

"Bon Jovi isn't as good as they used to be," he says.

She snorts without a trace of humor in her voice, the sound short and clear as a gavel's knock. She puts the magazine in the bed stand drawer. What could she possibly be looking for? Burns wonders. Shorter? Longer? A different color? Ten, fifteen years ago this would be incredibly titillating news, the prospect of a blond or a redhead astride him. Now he is just puzzled. What's she thinking? Is this one of those pregnant things, like a craving?

She turns on the television. "Oh my god," she says, bumping the volume. It is the show about the woman who arranges dates for millionaires. Burns stops, regards the bachelor. He is young, with a shaved head and eyes that are too close together. He looks like the witless son of a Bond villain. The matching lady is shouting something about flowers and romance. Rachel laughs and rubs her belly.

"It's all, like, programmed now," Burns says. "Even fucking Bon Jovi. It was like watching a Broadway show or something."

"Is he asleep?" she says. "Did he even stay awake for the whole thing? And, oh, by the way, my water didn't break. So thanks for asking."

"I mean it was like the *Lion King* or something," Burns says. "And when I saw you here in bed I had a pretty good idea that your water didn't break. Do we even have extra sheets around here anymore, anyway?"

"That's what you're worried about?" she says.

"I have a meeting tomorrow," Burns says. It is his trump card. Ever since Rachel quit copywriting to stay at home with Tyler, even though he was in full-time daycare and then school, any work-related pretense has been rock solid, and Burns knows that he has been using it as a crutch. Like an aging basketball player with one good move left in him, he knows there will come a time, very soon, when that one move doesn't work anymore, when Rachel will smack it right back in his face with the newborn. How long does he have? Two weeks? Four?

Rachel turns her attention back to the television. There is a new millionaire now. This one is older, with obvious plastic surgery. He looks like a Ken doll's father.

"I have to meet Julie tomorrow," he says. And this meeting is important. Could be important. Could be, he is well aware, the last meeting he ever has as an employee of the company.

"Tell her I said hi," Rachel says.

Tell her Rachel said hi, Burns thinks, while I'm getting fired. Or not fired. Promoted maybe? Unlikely, not with the economy, not with the company consolidating offices all over the place. He has heard of plenty layoffs and no promotions. But, still, he is a good employee. Not great, but good. Serviceable, reliable. Maybe the kind of guy they would want to move along in this kind of climate?

Maybe they just want to cut his salary. How bad are things, he thinks, when you're hoping for just a salary cut? He doesn't want to think about exactly what getting fired would mean. Would they be able to keep the house? Health insurance? What the hell is COBRA, anyway? How many mortgage payments can you miss?

Where the fuck would he get his Adderall?

"I'll have to leave early," Burns says, "get into the city in time."

Rachel turns up the volume on the television.

Burns is suddenly starving and he heads for the kitchen. Tyler is asleep already. The concert was a terrible idea. The last time he saw Bon Jovi was twenty years ago, and he was drunk and high, young and stupid. Unburdened. Bon Jovi had seemed like a perfect mix between rock and pop—hard enough for the bikers, but soft enough for their girlfriends. A party for everybody. It had that feeling that the great rock shows had, like anything could happen, like something was going to happen, something important and fun and transcendent, something they would all remember for the rest of their lives. That is what he remembers: the feeling that something was going to happen. It's a feeling he had often, then, in his twenties. Something was going to happen. Something good. Important and big. And he, Burns, was going to be in the middle of it all, like Jack Kerouac or Ken Kesey or at least Tom Wolfe or Hunter Thompson. He wonders if they knew it at the time, if Kerouac and Cassidy had that same feeling that Burns had at the Bon Jovi show all those years ago: everything is opening up, anything can happen, and I'm going to be right in the middle of it all.

What was the thing from *Almost Famous*? It's all happening. If there's a real Penny Lane, he thinks, she's sucking oxygen in some state-funded nursing home right now. Would she look back on those days of everything happening, of spinning from city to city in a rock and roll haze, and smile, knowing that it wasn't happening anymore but at least she lived her life? Or would she curse those days, the smoking and drinking, fooling around, focus on the paths not chosen and how they might have led to a more graceful ending.

The old Penny Lane would have been horrified by what he saw last night. It was like some kind of Super Bowl halftime show—everything scripted down to the second. He's not even sure if Bon Jovi was really singing, if that was really Richie Sambora or a hologram projected onto the stage. It could have been Justin Bieber himself in a wig and torn jeans, or the touring Broadway version of The Bon Jovi Concert Experience.

"Hey Buddy! Great show, huh?" Shit. Seacrest.

"Oh god," Burns says.

"They rocked it out, daddy-o!" Seacrest says.

"They did not rock it out," Burns whispers. He counts to ten. Sometimes this works, sometimes it doesn't. Outside, he can hear cars, people shouting. They were going to move to a better neighborhood before the baby, but then the recession hit and now this meeting tomorrow. Thank god for procrastination, Burns thinks.

"Oh they rocked the house, guy!" Seacrest says. "Maybe it's been too long since your last rock and roll show. Maybe you needed some of that good stuff you like so much to really, as the hippies used to say, open yourself up to the experience."

Burns opens a bottle of wine. Sometimes this works, too.

"Seacrest out!" the voice says. Goddamit, Burns thinks. He doesn't even say that in real life anymore.

"That show did not fucking rock," Burns whispers, terse, like a scolding, but there's nobody else in the room. He takes a deep drink of the wine and listens for an answer. Nothing. Hah. He takes another drink.

"That show did not rock," he says again, softer.

And Tyler. Tyler fidgeted, held his hands over his ears, cried when Burns refused to leave before the encore, which was, of course, "Wanted Dead or Alive." The boy loosened up for just a moment, during the group sing-a-long—"and I'm wanted, waaaaanted, dead or alive"—but when the lights came up and the music stopped, Burns wasn't sure whether he was excited about the song, about the fleeting magic of singing along with twenty thousand people, or about going home.

It was loud and raucous and yet somehow absolutely safe, like they were filming a rock show in a made-for-TV movie. Burns is getting a little buzzed now. He opens his phone and thumbs through the music. He wonders if his vinyl is still in the basement. Or the attic. Or the storage unit. He's pretty sure they didn't throw them all away, but he remembers moving and doesn't remember any milk crates full of albums.

He finds *Exile On Main Street* and hits play. Mick Jagger sings:

I hear you talkin' when I'm on the street.
Your mouth don't move but I can hear you speak.
What's the matter with the boy?
He don't come around no more.
Is he checking out for sure?
Is he gonna close the door on me...

There are all kinds of ways to interpret that, Burns thinks. Still, kind of weird, actually.

"Good tune," Seacrest says.

"What would you know about it?" Burns asks.

"It's no 'Baby,' but still," Seacrest says.

"I can't believe I know the name of that song," Burns says.

Seacrest laughs. "Seacrest out," he says. Burns can hear the sympathy in his voice. So now his own subconscious is feeling sorry for him.

Burns finishes the wine, pours another glass. "I can't even feel the pain no moooooore," Mick Jagger sings. Burns turns it up.

Burns is still a little drunk. He gets to the coffee shop early, eats two breakfast sandwiches, drinks an entire bottle of water and two espressos. He's nervous. Not about meeting Julie, but about what might happen next. He's heard the rumors—downsizing, rightsizing, consolidating offices, just plain old laying people off. He's got a pregnant wife and a son in private school, a pile of credit cards racking up a bigger pile of debt, a home equity line of credit that seemed like a good idea when the market was going gangbusters. Selling pharmaceuticals in the Maryland suburbs is all he's ever done, and he's not even that good at it.

It's ten forty-five and Julie is late, which is neither disappointing nor out of the ordinary. Burns checks his email and looks around the coffee shop. He's read the sports page twice already. He scans the paper. The Democrats are mad at the president. The Republicans are mad at everybody. The wars are going badly. How many wars are there, even? Everything is getting worse, and what the hell can anybody do about any of it?

He looks around. It is too bright in here. Too clean. Too much like all the other Starbucks everywhere. Burns is still getting used to this kind of coffee shop, with its pierced attendants and scones, comfy chairs and coffee sizes that sound like made-up words. Burns refuses to use the word *venti*. He orders a large and takes what they give him—sometimes this is the largest size, sometimes the one he knows they actually call a grande. He is slightly embarrassed to even know any of these words.

He isn't used to the city anymore. All of these people must get their clothes in the same place. Their pants are too tight and their t-shirts look like the ones Ryan Seacrest and Justin Bieber wear, the ones that look like they came out of a dumpster but also like they cost as much as a car payment. These people are too young and too attractive. They are graphic designers and bike messengers and the CEOs of dot-com startups. Like extras in an HBO sitcom. Who the fuck are these people? They have time on a Tuesday to sit here and type. To text? To linger in comfy chairs and drink five dollar coffee? By this time of day, Burns would have had at least two appointments and be driving to his third. Why aren't they at work, in offices?

Of course, Burns hasn't worked in an office in years, not since the first slowdown in the nineties. He remembers his old office—window, couch, a place to put all the papers and samples and trinkets they were handing out to doctors back then. It was fun, like a natural extension of college. It felt like what it was supposed to feel like – a bunch of good-looking twenty-somethings hanging out, talking about *Melrose Place* and *Beverly Hills 90210*, the Redskins, the new bands, about what they did the night before and how to cure a hangover and what they were going to be doing over the weekend, about 401Ks, stock tips, what to do with all the money they were all making all of the sudden.

Burns realizes that he's never felt as well off as he did when he was twenty-six. It was that feeling: anything could happen.

And the tech boom was a land grab. A gold rush. They were right in the middle of a new industrial revolution. One day, nobody had ever heard of email, Yahoo, Google. The next day, everybody was talking about IPOs like they were as common as five-dollar bills. Even in pharmaceuticals, it seemed like everything was changing, like everybody was going to be rich and anybody who wasn't using their money to make more money was some kind of hillbilly. Burns shakes his head. And now here he is, still working the same job, waiting for Julie to tell him if he's going to be able to keep working the same job, or maybe some slightly worse or worse-paying variation of it, or no job at all. Julie who he trained when she was fresh out of college. Julie with her vice president's title, her BMW and beach house and perky tits unaffected by childrearing.

He feels his love handles spilling over his Dockers, rubs a hand over his face. Opening the second bottle of wine was a really bad idea.

He feels the pills in his pockets. Snorting some Adderall right before he meets with Julie would be an even worse idea.

To his left, three young men in tech worker blue button-downs are talking about server space limitations the way men of Burns' father's generation once talked about shortstops and war bonds. They are young, barely out of college, with elaborately messy hairstyles that Burns imagines took an hour to get just right. He can picture them there in the morning, twisting and ruffling and perhaps tousling one another's hair until it reaches that perfect state of coiffed unkemptness. It is, like so much about these people, completely confounding and ridiculous, and when he tries it he realizes that he doesn't even know what kind of product you'd need to achieve this state. When Tyler is getting his hair cut at the mall, Burns stares at the hundreds of bottles, tries to decipher the names and uses, and he can't even figure out which are for men and which are for women and if there's even a difference anymore.

"It just won't be able to handle it!" one of them shouts, and the lawyer at the next table shoots him a look. Burns wonders about how much they seem to care about this stuff. Did he ever care about anything enough to raise his voice? He remembers meetings. People with opinions. A time when he was one of those people. But still, has he ever so much as raised his voice? And why would he? Why would anybody care that much? At the end of the day, everybody is pushing widgets, just trying to get through eight hours without getting hassled. Just trying to get through the fiscal year to another chance to take a week off at some overpriced summer rental that his wife will complain about anyway.

He feels dim. Numb. Really should have just had a few hits of the stuff this morning. Coffee can't hold a candle to it. He is considering moving to the bathroom when Julie appears out of nowhere, sits down with a giant mug of cappuccino. Burns stands.

"Please," she says, in that down-to-earth, self-deprecating way that Burns thinks might actually be real. He's watched doctors drool over Julie for a decade now, and he knows this is her professional demeanor. He knows it works—on doctors, nurses, on corporate, on him. "How's Rachel?" she says. "Tyler?"

"What?" Burns says. Should have just snorted a little bit, he thinks.

"Your eight-months-pregnant wife and nine-year-old son?" she says.

Julie is good with people, never misses a detail. He's been telling himself for years that he needs to be more like this, has even, on occasion, started taking notes, making crib sheets, but it never really takes.

"They're fine, great," he says, thinking, Rachel either hates me or doesn't give a shit, and Tyler is obsessed with a young, androgynous male pop star, and soon we'll have another baby to feed and clothe and pay for college and I'm pretty sure you're going to fire me, but all I can think about is I'm sorry I didn't notice when you came in here because I'd like to get a look at your ass today.

"Everything's hunky dory," he says. "Cool, I mean. Everything is cool."

"Well, I'm going to just cut to the chase and be honest with you," she says. "Because we've known each other a long time."

"Okay," he says. Maybe the wine was actually a good idea. It might be better to be a little drunk for this conversation. Just a little bump of Adderall, maybe. "We're consolidating our offices across the region. I'm losing half my people. The recession is killing us, and the new regulations make it a lot easier to bring sales online."

Burns nods. He can feel his bladder filling up, the bile in the back of his throat. His breath tastes like sausage. Why can't I ever remember to bring goddam mints, he thinks. Forty-three years old and I can't remember to bring a mint to a meeting with my boss.

Julie is still talking. "So there are two ways this can go," she says. She pauses and for just a second he sees real uncertainty in her eyes. He is fired. He knows it. "You can get two months severance, then unemployment. Which is not a bad deal, even though I know it doesn't sound like a good one. It's better than what some people are getting. Or you could make the move and do pretty much the same job, for a slightly reduced salary, in Scranton/Wilkes-Barre."

Burns has to go to the bathroom. Too much coffee. Too much water. Scranton? His bladder is burning, erupting. A quick snort, maybe, is all he needs to get through this conversation.

"Scranton/Wilkes-Barre?" he says.

"Yes," Julie says. And then, "Are you okay?"

"Pennsylvania."

"That is where it is. Like, well, I shouldn't say this, you know, it's not going to make you feel much better. That's where *The Office* is set."

"Corporate? That office. What?"

"The television show."

"I have to go to the bathroom," he says.

"I understand," she says, and puts a hand over his. Her hands are so soft. Jesus, how can she keep them so soft? Burns thinks about Rachel's hands, swollen with the pregnancy, scaly with psoriasis. He stands, wobbles toward the bathroom. "Take as much time as you need," she says. "I'll be right here."

The bathroom is locked. Of course. He tries the women's, then knocks politely on the men's. "Busy," somebody calls. The voice is accented, carefree. The owner of that voice has all the time in the world for sitting in comfy chairs and drinking five dollar coffee.

"I have to fucking piss," Burns whispers through the door.

"Oh my," says the comfy chair-sitter.

Silence.

Burns knocks louder. "Come on, man," he says. Julie is looking at him with a mix of pity and bemusement. He waves. She is looking good today, he thinks. At this age, it's so obvious who has and hasn't had children.

He is in pain, as if his bladder is filled with scalding hot coffee. He is sweating, is aware of his face turning red. Nothing would feel better than going to the bathroom right now. Bathroom then a nice long snort. He can feel the burning in his nose, the aftertaste slipping down the back of his throat. He knocks again. Julie is pecking at her iPhone. Scranton? He was ready for worse, but Scranton? Maybe he could take the severance, find something he really likes doing, open up a coffee shop, one with room for more than one person in the goddam bathroom. Maybe he could start a website, learn HTML, get some startup money and hire those server guys in the corner. Maybe he could sit around the house in his underwear, get fatter, watch his little retirement wither until it blows away, bit by bit. Maybe he could change diapers until there isn't a house anymore and they are living in the car, or in Rachel's mother's basement in Central Pennsylvania.

He knocks on the door again. "Occupied," says the voice.

Occupied, Burns thinks. Who says *occupied*?

He has to do something. Julie is still watching. He fingers the pill in his pocket. And before he thinks about it he is pushing through the emergency exit, the sounds of the city spiraling all around him in this alleyway. He leans against the wall and lets it go, the feeling one of pure relief. He lets out a groan, is looking around for a place to grind up the pill when he feels the tap on his shoulder.

"Sir?" It is the flat voice of a policeman. He knows from the tone that the guy is young. Can hear his car now, idling behind them.

"Sir. I'm going to have to ask you to put away your penis and turn around. In that order, please." Because of course a man pissing in an alley at eleven o'clock in the morning would need directions this specific.

Burns does as told.

"Have you been drinking?" the cop asks. Burns was right. He is young. Add a piercing and a messenger bag, some extravagantly mussed hair, and he could have been any of the people from the coffee shop.

"I was just in a business meeting," Burns says. "The bathroom was busy. My boss was late. I had a lot of coffee."

He wants to hit the young officer, wants to hit the wall, keep on hitting until his hand is a useless bloody pulp and then start in with his forehead. He wants this to be somebody else's fault. He is doing his best for his family, for himself, Julie, the company. This is the thanks he gets: a kid arresting him on a busy street while some comfy chair-sitter sings "Occupied" from behind a locked door. He wants to smash the comfy chair-sitter's head into the espresso machine. He wants to be twenty again. To have his entire life in front of him and this little departure would be a funny story told at a party later, at a bar, at work washing dishes or waiting tables. He wants anything but this. He wonders if the District Police take Discover, if he'll actually be thrown in jail. Does Leon have a car? Would he drive into the city? Would Julie bail him out? Rachel? And what if she goes into labor while he is locked up in the District jail with god knows who? If they frisk him, they're going to find the Adderall. Julie is right inside.

Scranton?

"Please follow me, sir," the cop says. He leads Burns into the back of the police car and writes a citation. "Public urination, sir," he says. "We frown on it here in the District of Columbia."

A knock on the window. Julie. "What the fuck is happening here?" she says.

"This man with you?" the cop says.

For a second, Burns has a small burst of pride. Yes, he is with her. Maybe that will make a difference. Look at her.

"Yes," Julie says. "What's the problem, officer?"

"Public urination," the cop says. "We just have to give your *friend* here a citation. He'll be free to go in a few minutes."

Julie raps on the back window of the cruiser. "I think we better talk later," she says. "Think about what I said before."

"Justin whowhat now?" Leon says. He rubs his goatee, leans his bulk back in the chair. "Jesus Christ, Burns." He finishes his beer and drops the can on the floor, reaches for another one.

"It's..." Burns starts.

"I mean. Is that the kid I think it is?"

"The hair?" Burns says.

"For fuck's sake, man. What's going on over there?" He points the neck of his guitar toward Burns' house, glowing yellowy dark through the hedges. He shakes his head, as if this latest thing is just another in the long line of things—poor lawn maintenance, lack of basic plumbing skills, the propensity to hire third parties for home improvement projects large and small, the fact that Tyler dropped out of guitar lessons after three sessions and wasn't "man enough" to do it to Leon's face, and any number of unspoken failings that Burns is not actually aware of—that indicate both Burns' personal insufficiency and the larger "pussifiction of America."

"What's that supposed to mean?" Burns says. Lately, he's been trying this tactic, a shot across the bow before Leon can get started.

Leon plays the first few lines to "Bell Bottom Blues" and Burns is amazed, as always, at his neighbor's skill. How can you just pull that out of nowhere? It's incredible, a miracle. And it is criminal that this man, who once played for a band that toured with the Animals, who taught guitar lessons for thirty years at the community college until being rightsized—a pussy word if there ever was one—at the very beginning of the recession, is now in such a precarious position. Like a canary in a coalmine, Leon is in danger of foreclosure, and as they sit there in the living room, a stack of ponderous notices and bills and notes of sale from at least four different companies serve as a treacherous coaster for an array of Natural Light cans.

How can a guy with talent like this be sitting here, playing like that, and still be so badly in debt that next month he could be living out of his car? And these pop stars nowadays. Lady Gaga is riffing on Marilyn Manson's lousy script and shocking people all the way to the bank. That butterface Fergie is playing at the Super Bowl. It is literally impossible to go a day without hearing anything about Billy Ray Cyrus' daughter, the one with the television show that Tyler watches. Burns still can't figure out that show. Sometimes she's famous and sometimes she's not? Sometimes she's some normal girl and sometimes she's Hannah Montana? Real housewives are cutting singles. And Bieber! Justin Bieber is a global sensation. Last night Burns watched the Letterman show. In the Heisman Trophy winner's list of "Top Ten Things I Can Tell You Now" was, "I'll admit it. I have Bieber Fever."

Leon finishes a beer and hands another one to Burns.

"I'm just saying, is all," Leon says.

"He's fine. Tyler is fine."

When I was that age, I was already chasing pussy," Leon says.

"He's nine," Burns says.

"What I said," Leon says. "Shit, at nine? Boy you should have seen me. I was all up in it."

"Leon," Burns says. "That's actually, that's just kind of gross."

Leon grunts in a way that sounds like his point has just been proven. Burns feels it coming again. He wants something to happen. Something big, maybe even something bad. He remembers the days after 9/11, a hazy, scary time when it seemed inappropriate to do anything other than watch television and drink and obsess endlessly about the horror of what had just happened. It was like time stood still, the regular rules no longer applied—there was no worrying about details, about who did what or whether your timesheets were submitted, whether inventory matched sales records or whether sales matched projections. It was terrible, of course, but still, when he thinks about it, he doesn't think about those poor souls jumping out of the towers, the doomed firemen running into burning buildings. He thinks about sitting around the house, watching the towers slowly imploding on his television again and again and again, and, for once, not worrying about a goddam thing.

His stomach turns and he has to pee again. He drinks from his warm beer and fights the involuntary urge to throw up.

"You wouldn't believe what I saw today," Leon says.

Burns glances at his watch. It is far too seldom that he is able to talk to another man, share a few beers, bitch about home life and the Redskins and the pussification of America. But he knows that he will believe what Leon saw today, that what he saw was most likely something on Fox News. Leon is a reformed hippie, ashamed now that he was in the mud at Woodstock, that he once lived for a month on Kesey's farm. It was 9/11 that did it, flipped some kind of switch that must have been waiting to be turned on for some time, as the form of his golden years began to crystallize into a steady shunting aside and decomposition.

"They are marrying queers in the state of Massachusetts," Leon says. "I saw it with my own eyes. Two men, standing there in matching tuxes, saying the same vows you said with your lovely wife however many years ago."

Burns finishes his beer, slaps Leon on the leg. "Thanks, buddy," he says. "But I gotta roll."

"Watch out for that Bieber shit!" Leon says.

Burns sneaks into Tyler's room and sits on his bed. Is this crazy? Only if you look at it in a certain way. It's not too late to bail out. He can simply take off his shoes, throw his clothes in the closet, and crawl into bed like any other night.

"What are you doing, Dad?" Tyler says. Burns sits. He yawns. It is a good question, one he's not sure he's ready to answer.

Tyler yawns. "I was sleeping," he says.

Burns looks at the clock on the wall—the garish plastic image of Justin Bieber glowing 10:25. When Burns was Tyler's age, he had a Boston Celtics alarm clock. "I was thinking we might get ourselves a midnight snack," he says. "Ice cream?"

The boy doesn't speak, but follows Burns out to the car. He is wearing sweatpants and a Justin Bieber t-shirt. Burns carries Tyler's Chuck Taylor's, a birthday present he doesn't yet wear, and a black hooded sweatshirt to the car.

He wonders if Rachel will wake up, come looking for them. If she will call his cell, text, contact the local hospitals and police station. Or if she would simply shrug and turn on the television and waddle to the kitchen for another pint of Cherry Garcia.

Burns drives slowly—he has snorted three more lines of Adderall and he feels like he could dunk a basketball, but he is most likely still a little drunk from the beers at Leon's house.

Tyler is sitting in the passenger seat, eyes closed. His hair looks positively Bieberish—a feathery halo, like a girl imitating the early Beatles. Is this kidnapping, he wonders? But it can't be kidnapping if it's already your own kid, right? But there are those guys who do get arrested for kidnapping, busted trying to sneak a seven year old into Paris or holed up in some Quality Inn outside Tallahassee.

Those guys are divorced already, though, late on payments, deep into a domestic police situation. The thing today—public urination—that doesn't connote a police record, right? It's not good, certainly, but not necessarily Child Protective Services bad. The kind of thing, though, that could show up in divorce proceedings.

Burns has pondered divorce and the idea provokes a quick stab of freedom and then the freefall of total failure, almost exactly the way he felt after the meeting with Julie.

He drives past a Starbucks and then another, past the chic little suburban nightspots that he and Rachel once frequented, stays on Connecticut Avenue past the dark office towers and apartments that have cropped up everywhere, encroaching, connecting the entire region in one mass of overly planned communities. He looks at Tyler's hair again. What kind of boy... he starts. But, no, tonight will be good. This is what they need. What Tyler needs, maybe what Burns needs. This is a little male bonding, like when his uncles used to take him to Dietle's Tavern to play pinball while they drank beer and smoked and complained about the Redskins or the Senators, or when he used to kick around the gym, shooting baskets and trying not to get run over while his dad played pickup with the rest of the guys on his shift.

He drives down Connecticut, takes a left onto U, and parks along a side street. Tyler is still sleeping and he wakes the boy gently.

"Ice cream?" Tyler says.

"I had another idea," Burns says. "Let's go see some music."

The boy actually starts crying, tries to get back into the car, and Burns has to carry him a block before the Tyler will walk under his own power again.

"Are we going to the same place as last night?" Tyler says.

"No way buddy," Burns says. "Between me and you? That kind of sucked. Tonight we're going to see some real music."

"Like Justin?" Tyler says. If only he didn't use just the first name, Burns thinks. Maybe he could stomach the whole thing.

"No, not quite," Burns says. "You know the band we listen to in the car sometimes? The ones who sing the 'uh oh oh' song? The 'Stay Positive' song? It's those guys. They're here, and we're really lucky we have a chance to go see them."

"I want to see Justin," Tyler says, as if Burns has just denied him a cupcake.

"And we will," Burns says. "Sometime. I promise. I just want you to see some other music before then, too. Okay?"

"Justin is here soon," Tyler says. "I heard on the radio." And then, "this is scary."

"Oh, there's nothing to be scared of," Burns says. Although there is plenty to be scared of, like the pack of teenagers loitering outside the Latino Mercado that they're moving past right now. A few of them say something in Spanish and Burns bites the inside of his cheek, squeezes Tyler's hand. He can see the club up ahead of them. He hasn't been here for what, ten years? Fifteen? It looks the same. Finally, Burns thinks, something that actually looks the same.

They wait in line with a few hundred guys wearing baseball hats and thermal underwear with t-shirts over top. Burns feels self-conscious about his own striped button down and khakis. Should have changed. Should keep a t-shirt and jeans in the car, just for this kind of thing.

One thing Burns notices right away: Tyler is the only kid here, the youngest by about fourteen years. He realizes that most of these guys are closer to Tyler's age than his own. This is not cool.

But Tyler's crazy for the Hold Steady, or he was for a while there. Every time they would drive to Target or a play date he would request it: "Daddy, put on 'uh oh oh.'"

That was before the Bieber came floating down out of wherever it came from, bubbling in through the water for all Burns knows. Better days. Everything is getting worse, even for these kids standing around here in their obscure t-shirts and scuffed baseball hats, smoking their Marlboro Reds, already drunk from a few beers after work. Everything is already getting worse for Tyler, who has traded the shouted poetry and power chords of the Hold Steady for the whispery pop confection of Justin Bieber. Everything. All the time.

Finally they get to the front and Burns hands the ticket printouts to the bouncer. He's a big kid, six-four or five, three hundred pounds at least, with a thing in his nose and saucers that stretch out his ears like a Brazilian tribesman.

"What's this?" he says.

He waves a hand at Tyler like Burns is trying to bring in a keg or a horse.

"Two dudes. Two tickets," he says.

"No, no, no," the bouncer says.

"What?"

"I'm not even sure, man, but you can't bring that kid in here. Not on my shift, dude," he says. "I mean...shouldn't he be, like, asleep? Kids need their sleep, man."

"He had a big nap this afternoon," Burns says. He is getting parenting advice from the doorman at the 9:30 Club?

The line is piling up and Burns hears grumbling behind him.

Then a skinny man who looks like Patti Smith arrives. The bouncer looks relieved.

"Oh no," Patti Smith says. "No way. No fucking way." He's got a thick New York accent and Burns wonders for just a moment whether this really could be Patti Smith. Or one of the Ramones. "I don't even know what the fuck you're thinking, man," the guy says.

"You don't have to swear in front of the kid," Burns says, but already he's backing up, pulling Tyler along the sidewalk. He can hear the opening strains of "Boys and Girls in America" and they stand there on the street for a few minutes, listening to the muted rock with a line of smokers along the wall.

"That's what it's all about, son," Burns say. "Rock and roll." It feels stupid coming out of his mouth. He is sweating through his button-down.

"Are we going to get ice cream now?" Tyler says. "Can we listen to Justin on the way home?"

Burns sighs. He takes the boy's hand in his. "Yes. Yes we can," he says.

Burns tucks the boy into bed and fumbles in the pantry until he finds a bottle of Maker's Mark. Rachel is sleeping soundly. If he is lucky, Tyler won't say anything at all about their little excursion, or Rachel won't hear him when he does.

He walks to the sliding glass door, peeks out at Leon's house glowing bright beyond the bushes. It is midnight. Leon is moving back and forth between the yard and the house, lugging great bags full of something, spilling them into a makeshift fire pit he has created by disassembling a rock wall that once marked the borders between his and the neighbor's garden. Burns opens the door and walks quietly through the yard, watching while the old man shakes out a garbage bag full of envelopes.

"What the hell are you doing?" Burns says.

Leon stops, looks up slowly. He smiles. The old man is wearing a tie-dye and shorts and he looks more like Jerry Garcia than ever. "Well," he says. "If the government is going to get this house, I'm gonna damn sure not leave 'em anything would make it easy for them to, you know, steal my identity or somesuch. I know how worried everybody is nowadays about our precious identities."

Leon stumbles back toward the house and Burns regards the yard. Scattered everywhere are letters—bills, junk mail, solicitations. He picks one up. It is an unopened Visa bill from 1994.

"The fuck are you doing?" Burns says as Leon limps over with his gas can. Burns looks back at his own house, dark and quiet. He wonders if he left the door open. Maybe. Probably not.

"The fuck does it look like I'm doing?" Leon says.

"Like you're going to burn the whole fucking neighborhood down," Burns says.

The voice of Ryan Seacrest pops into his head: "burnin' down the house!"

"Not funny!" Burns shouts. Leon is slopping gas everywhere, the smell pushing up into Burns' nose.

"No shit it's not funny," Leon says. "Serious as a heart attack. As a fucking suicide."

"Wait a minute," Burns says. "You're not gonna kill yourself here, are you?"

Leon pauses, looks at Burns as if he has answered a math problem terribly wrong. He shakes his head. "He just never quite gets it," Leon says. "No, asshole. I'm not taking my life. I'm goddam saving it."

"Watch out!" Seacrest's voice says. "You might get what you're after!"

"Jesus Christ," Burns says.

"I think he might have bigger fish to fry," Leon says. He looks at the perimeter of his makeshift fire pit. "And, besides, fuck him."

Burns runs back to his house. He opens the sliding glass door, takes the fire extinguisher from its place in the pantry, then runs back to Leon's yard.

"Okay," he says.

"Okay what?" Leon says.

Burns nods at the fire pit. "Let's see what happens next."

"We got tickets!" Tyler says.

Burns looks to Rachel, but she is already in the bathroom.

"What?" he says.

"Justin!" Tyler says, and Burns cringes. "The concert! Tonight! Oh my god," he says. "I can't believe it. I'm so excited, Dad. Thanks so much for taking me."

"Where is it?" Burns says, then thinks, what? "Thanks for taking you?" he says.

Rachel lumbers out of the bathroom and plops onto the couch. "I can't exactly take him," she says, gesturing to her belly.

"I'm taking him to see Justin Bieber?" Burns says. He has as much control over this situation, he thinks, as he does over whether or not the dentist needs to fill a cavity. "Tonight?"

"Oh, did you have big plans?" Rachel says. "Were you and Leon gong to drink beer and play guitars?"

"No," Burns says. "Maybe. Kind of. I need—"

"Or maybe light a big, dangerous, illegal fire in his back yard. Endanger your son and your wife and your unborn child?"

Is there anything he can say about work, about making all the money? Could he actually tell her the truth? No, she won't, couldn't understand the truth. And the truth is that it was beautiful, wonderful, that Burns and the old guitar player passed around a bottle of whiskey and watched every single piece of paper that had Leon's name on it burn. They watched as night became day and then smoldered back into night. And for just a glimmer, Burns felt it again, that feeling like anything could happen, like whatever what happening next was going to be amazing.

"Have you showered?" Rachel asks. "You smell like a bonfire." She rubs her belly, turns on the television. "It starts at eight," she says. "You probably don't want to be late."

Burns opens a beer and goes into the bathroom. When they painted the office light blue and re-assembled the crib, Burns was forced to retreat further, first to the patio and then, due to the cold weather, to this room. It is yellowing, dusty, dirty. He is not sure when the floor was last cleaned. He sits down on the toilet with his beer and laptop, pulls down his pants out of habit as much as anything else, and clicks open his email. Julie wants him to call. This cannot be good. This is the first he's heard from her since yesterday, and he pictures her afternoon as a string of urgent meetings with Human Resources and Legal. *If we fire him, do we have to pay a severance? What if he got a public urination citation during the meeting? What if his Adderall supplies haven't quite balanced out for the last six months?*

Adderall. He crushes up four pills, snorts a third of the powder, and puts the rest into his mini-Altoid container. A Justin Bieber concert? This is a worst-case scenario. He pictures Tyler screaming along with ten thousand twelve-year-old girls, screaming for another boy, a boy with that haircut. It is too much to bear. He has to do something. For Tyler. For all of them. He finishes the beer and picks up a yoga magazine. He stares at the cover. An impossibly skinny old man is bent into an unlikely position. His face is set in what Burns assumes is supposed to be a look of wisdom. But what he looks like is scared. This old man is how many years from dying? How long will all this yoga extend his life? Does he eat meat? Drink alcohol? Does he crunch ADHD medicine into a powder and suck it up his nose?

And still, Burns thinks, this is guy is dying, too. Same as the rest of us.

"Whoa, buddy. It's getting a little dark in here!" Ryan Seacrest's voice seems magnified today, produced. It is smooth and flawless. "That's some deep stuff there, buddy. Really trippy."

"Bite me," Burns says.

"He's got one for everything, people!" Seacrest says.

Burns puts his head in his hands. The bathroom smells like shit and mildew. His stomach is churning, pulling in on itself. He wonders how long it would take for him to fast his way to better abs, like those people on *Survivor*. They all wind up looking terrible, too skinny and malnourished, like stray dogs in some third world country, but there's a point in the middle there where they just look like J. Crew models.

Burns sticks his fingers in his ears. This has to stop. Ryan Seacrest? Justin Bieber? *Real Housewives* and Bravo Andy? What is wrong in this house? They are all possessed, each of them.

"Something's gotta give, right?" Seacrest says. His voice is soft. Burns looks around the little room to make sure there's not somebody actually there with him. This is the first time Seacrest, his Seacrest, has sounded like anything other than a flamboyant radio deejay from *Happy Days*.

"We must protect this house!" the voice screams. It is Ryan Seacrest amplified by twenty. He jumps. The laptop slaps to the floor, skitters under the vanity. Burns balances on one leg, hops, hops again, struggling to regain his balance. He feels for the towel rack, leans, and the entire thing goes down. Burns is laying flat on his belly with the towel rack tight in his hands. It is silent except for the sound of his own panting. He rolls over, looks at the stains on the ceiling, cobwebs in the corners.

Why is Ryan Seacrest imitating an UnderArmour commercial? Then again, he is right. That's what it's all about. That's what being a man is all about. That is the lesson he has to teach Tyler before it's too late. We must protect this house. Like Leon, misguided as he might be. That's all he was trying to do, and it was beautiful, transfixing. We must protect this house. And that means work, that means Julie, that means Rachel and the baby and Tyler.

That means everything.

For the second time in two days, Burns is absolutely sure about what he has to do.

Burns takes a hit and tries to hold the smoke in this time. Again, his stomach roils and his head spins and the cough seems to come from somewhere deep inside him, from his balls, from wherever it was that ancient people believed the soul resides. The cough is like a sneeze in fast motion, a quick build up and then a second until the inevitable release. He realizes he is laughing, giggling, tears running down his face.

For a moment he is gone—head pleasantly smoggy, giggling, coughing, tears and snot and a full bladder and the idea of pissing his pants is hilarious—the words, pissing his pants. He remembers a kid, elementary school, scrawny and needy. *Pisspants,* that was his name. And the name starts him off again. Pisspants. Fucking hilarious. "Pisspants," he says.

"Keep after it," Leon says. "This young person pot is a sight different than the stuff y'all were smoking in the eighties."

That is right. He is in Leon's house, smoking Leon's pot, Leon's *young people* pot. It is four in the afternoon and Burns is smoking pot in a room full of boxes, each of them heavy and squat and unmarked. It smells like fireworks and old magazines.

Leon does a hit, holds it in. He strums a few chords, then exhales.

"What's this 'pisspants' you're giggling about?" he says. He is trying to be stern, grumpy old Leon, the Tea Party hippie, but like a lungful of smoke, he can't hold it, and he breaks into a grin. "Pisspants," he giggles. "That's fucking funny."

"So where do you even get this young people weed?" Burns says.

"I have students," Leon says. "Young guitar players have young people weed. As always."

"I've been snorting Adderall," Burns says. "For a few months now."

"Gotta love musicians," Leon says. "I've been in this house for twelve years and I have never once had to go looking for a pot connect."

"I have a whole case of it over there in the house," Burns says.

"Wait. What?" Leon says. "You've been snorting what?"

"Adderall," Burns says. "It's like an attention deficit drug. ADHD. The kids, they grind it up, snort it. It's fucking awesome."

"You got any?" Leon says.

Burns puts his little Altoid container on the table. "Thought you'd never ask," he says.

Burns pours some of the powder onto a saucer.

"It's orange," Leon says.

"It is," Burns says. "Somehow that makes it seem, like, not as druggy, or something?"

"Like snorting children's aspirin," Leon says.

"Or something," Burns says. He cuts a line with his Discover Card—$3,500 owed and the payment due in three days—and pushes the saucer toward Leon.

Leon bends and expertly snorts the line. He leans back, considers, like a sommelier swishing cabernet around his cheeks. "Not bad," he says. "Not exactly Peruvian marching powder, but not bad at all."

"Not exactly what?" Burns says.

"Jesus," Leon says. He leans back, rubs the bridge of his nose, snorts again. "You're really nowhere near as cool as I thought you were for awhile there."

Burns snorts and puts his head in his hands. It's a weird feeling, with the pot and the Adderall and the Busch they've been drinking since lunch. Weirder. He looks to the kitchen, dishes stacked up like a game of Jenga.

"How long now?" he asks.

"Who what now?" Leon blurts. He stands up.

"Until you have to be out of the house," Burns says.

"Fuck. Yeah. Three days."

"I read in *Rolling Stone*," Burns says, feeling the crispness from the Adderall settle in, firming up, "a lot of this stuff is bullshit, mistakes. These mortgage companies, they don't even know who owns what anymore, these things have been bought so many times. They don't have any of the paper. You get yourself a lawyer, you go to court, you could—"

"A lawyer," Leon says. He pronounces it *law-yur*. He laughs. "I pay some pussy in a suit to help the bank rape me, to hold the dildo while they get it lined up with my asshole?"

"Lined up with your asshole," Burns says. "That's pretty good." He giggles. It is three hours until the Justin Bieber concert. He is probably fired. But still, he thinks, at least he has the house, Rachel, Tyler, the unborn child. God he loves his unborn child. He wants to do something for it right now, right this very instant, head out and kill something, build something, put something big and permanent in between it, whatever it is going to be, and the cold, shitty, decaying world it is going to find.

Leon is pacing. The energy in the room has changed. Burns opens another beer, hands one to Leon. The older man knocks the beer from his hand and watches as it pours onto a pile of *Washington Times* newspapers.

"*Rolling Stone*," Leon says." He read it in the *Rolling Stone*." He says it like he is saying the most ridiculous thing in the world, like Jon Stewart delivering a punch line.

Maybe the Adderall was not such a great idea. Burns stands. It is getting dark outside. He can see his house in the distance, the old windows cloudy from the inside. The hedges need to be trimmed and the rock patio they tried to put in a few years ago has gone slanted and dangerous, rocks pushing up at bad angles. It is a miracle Tyler has never fallen onto those rocks, hasn't impaled himself on the craggy surface. Who would just leave that there?

Leon is rooting around in the freezer. That's good, Burns thinks. A transition.

"I gotta go to that Justin Bieber concert tonight," he says. "Can you believe that?"

Leon grunts.

"I don't even know how I'm gonna drive," Burns says.

Leon pulls a box of eskimo pies out of the freezer. Then another. And another.

"You have a lot of eskimo pies, man," Burns says.

Finally Leon finds what he is looking for. A gun, flat and black, like the ones Burns has seen in the movies or on television. He lays it flat on the counter.

"What the fuck?" says Burns.

"Oh, I just gotta clean up around here. You know, in case these bank people are serious. Best to be ready, I suppose."

Burns is sitting on a beach. The water laps his bare feet. A drink is in his hand. He watches as his companion jogs in from a dip. It is Phoebe Cates. She smiles. "I didn't know," she says, and then she undoes the front of her bikini.

Do they even really work like that? In the front? In the background, The Cars' "Moving in Stereo" plays, sinister and sneaky. He knows this is a dream.

Still, those are amazing tits. Amazing tits.

She is opening up the door to the bathroom. Burns looks down. His pants are at his ankles. He is wearing a pirate costume—puffy shirt, pirate hat, pantaloons and boots. His eyepatch is around his neck. His penis is in his hand.

"Oh my god!" Phoebe Cates says.

Burns wakes up.

"Nice," his wife says. She nods at his crotch and Burns realizes he's massaging his penis through his khakis. "Moving in Stereo" is still playing in his head, along with a cackling that he suspects is Ryan Seacrest, but he can't even begin to deal with that now.

"Leon," he says.

"Whatever you're doing over there," she says. "Luckily for you, I actually, honestly, don't give a shit." She rubs her belly, pushes her hair behind her ears, and sits down next to him on the sofa. She smiles - kind, indulgent. It is the most generous thing she's done in months and Burns wells up, feels the lump in his throat again. What is happening to me? he thinks. It seems like he spends most days somewhere between wanting to smash his head against a windshield and bawl like a two year old. She puts a hand on his knee. "Julie called," she says. "She sounds—"

"I know," he says. "Don't worry, I'll..." and he has no idea what to say next. We must protect this house.

"I know," she says. "I know you will."

"We might have to move," he says. "To Scranton."

She runs a hand along his chest, pats him gently, and stands.

"Tyler's getting dressed," she says. "Thanks so much for taking him. I know, or, well, I have some kind of idea how much you don't really want to do this." She laughs. He realizes that he hasn't heard her really laugh for a long time.

"He's nine," Burns says. "It's fine." He sits up and is surprised to find that he doesn't feel bad. The young people pot knocked him out, but no hangover. A few orange pills and everything will be...but no, that's not how a grown man should deal with something like taking his nine-year-old to see his favorite singer. Best to just play this one straight, deal with it head-on, all of it: the screaming, the parking, the terrible lip-synced music and programmed dance routines, the eight-dollar Cokes and six-dollar popcorn.

It is a curse, a pox, but it is for Tyler.

He stands, stretches. "How does a grown man dress, you suppose," he asks his wife, "for a Justin Bieber concert?"

Burns is not the only man at the Justin Bieber concert. There are a few other wincing fathers here, escorting young sons. There are more gay men than he would have guessed. Of course, that's a whole other thing. He's surprised and pleased to find that this, the idea of it, the possibility that Tyler could be heading in that direction, doesn't bother him. Tyler is nine, and he could head any direction at all. Last year it was Harry Potter. Two years ago it was dinosaurs. Three years ago, trains. In a year, he could be walking around in a football helmet, or writing vampire novels, or skateboarding or painting water colors or chasing girls.

The lights go down and the sound is incredible. Twenty thousand tweens shrieking as one. The noise is a presence, a physical entity as tangible and near as a rainstorm. There's a charge in the arena that was missing from the Bon Jovi concert. It is electric. Tyler is shouting and laughing as Justin Bieber strides across the stage. The bass drum kicks. Burns is surprised that there are live musicians on stage. Somehow, he expected an *American Idol* situation—Bieber with a cordless microphone and pumped-in music, lip-syncing and counting his dance steps.

Almost against his will, Burns feels his feet tapping. He shouts "Woooooooooo!" and smiles, ruffles Tyler's hair. This is fun. He is having fun. He is having the most fun he's had in a long time and he is having it with his son at a Justin Bieber concert.

Bieber starts singing and every person in the arena seems to be singing along. Tyler shouts the words: "I'd wait on you forever and a day..." The girls to their right are massed into a group hug, crying, keening, singing and laughing. To the left, two young men hold hands and roll into one another, singing and smiling. Burns finds himself singing along: "whenever you smile, I smile." How does he even know the words? When did he learn this song? Of course, he's been listening to this album—is there only one?—through Tyler's door for the past six months.

The song ends and the sound comes back. It is a white noise unlike anything he's ever heard, a bright yellow noise—sharp, thick, with an energy that snaps like a thousand power lines.

The lights go down and a slow piano starts up. It's nice. This could be an Elton John song from the nineties—not the decade that Burns prefers, but still, this could be Elton John. Bieber starts singing and the yellow noise snaps back for a few seconds. The kid can sing. And he is singing. He's not lip-syncing. He moves across the stage with a practiced smoothness. He shakes hands in the front row. Behind him, suddenly, there's a waterfall.

My god, Burns thinks, this kid can do whatever he wants. Anything could happen.

Tyler is singing along and Burns feels like he's going to cry and he lets it happen, finally, allows himself to cry for just a brief moment. It comes out in a burst, a quick gasp of tears. He bawls once, twice, and then it's over. He wipes his eyes. Tyler reaches out and they are holding hands.

Bieber sings and floats across the floor. Behind him, twin screens as large as houses broadcast the action, switching expertly between the teen idol and his fans—front row, back row, girls and boys and moms and dads. Everybody knows the words. Most of them know the dances. Tyler is swaying side-to-side, singing, dancing. Burns sings. He still knows all the words. This would have been the most disturbing discovery two hours ago, but, right now, he's glad for it, barely aware of it, even, as he belts out lyrics about holding hands and new love and bounces lightly on his heels and squeezes Tyler's sweaty little hand.

The song finishes with a flourish and Burns shouts "Yes!" He flashes back to the summer he followed the Dead around for a week. This is not so much unlike that, he thinks. A crowd. A performer. Songs that everybody knows. He had connected with a blond from Colgate, spent the entire week getting high in her station wagon and tracking down menthol cigarettes in the parking lot and surrounding gas stations. He ate grilled cheese and slept beside the girl—what was her name?—and didn't so much as feel her breasts the entire week. It was before email, before Facebook. They sent a few letters and lost touch. She is probably the mother of five, married to a Wall Street trader. The one percent.

A guitar riff starts up and Bieber walks over to his guitarist, a guy who looks like a session musician, what Leon would call a *pro-fessional*, puts a hand to his ear, and then waves to the crowd.

Burns knows this song. He's heard it a million times pumping through Tyler's bedroom door.

"Here it is!" Tyler shouts. He grabs Burns in a quick hug and spins back toward the stage.

How did he not notice the guitar riff before? The way the drums snarl under that riff like a threat. It could be a Stones track. Okay, he thinks, an overproduced Stones track, but still.

He realizes that he's been at a concert for more than an hour and he hasn't heard Ryan Seacrest's voice once. Seacrest. Burns almost feels sorry for him. Burns doesn't know much about him, but he does know that he is famous for his workaholic tendencies. He is childless. Burns watches Tyler watch Justin Bieber. He waits, lets his mind go blank. Nothing.

Bieber swaggers around the stage. That's the word. There's a swagger to him. The kid is lucky if he weighs a hundred pounds. He has figure skater hair and he's probably wearing make-up and he's swaggering around the stage like Notorious B.I.G. or Iggy Pop. It is remarkable. Is that taught? Can it be?

Tyler is transfixed. He's smiling the little boy smile of pure, uncomplicated joy. Remember this, Burns thinks. Remember this, remember this, remember this.

Burns sees the lights before hears the sirens. It's a glow, a looping haze settled down over the neighborhood, poking through the trees, hanging over the rooftops. Something is wrong. Something is very, very wrong. Rachel, he thinks. The baby. He speeds up, squeals around the corner and is face to face with a battalion of police cars. A burly officer with a baby face waves him over. Burns rolls down his window.

"Can't get through here, sir," the officer says. "We have a disturbance. Stand off kind of situation."

"I live right there," Burns indicates his own house.

Tyler wakes up, rubs his eyes. "What's happening?" he says.

"Where?" the officer says.

"That house right there. 434," Burns says.

"You checked your cell phone tonight, sir?" the cop says.

"Battery died," Burns says.

"Please pull the car over here and come with me," the officer says. "He's been trying to reach you."

"Who?" Burns says, thinking, the doctor? The police? What the hell is the penalty for public urination, anyway?

"I need to check on my wife," Burns says. "She's—"

"We know," the cop says. "She's fine. There's somebody there with her."

"So who needs to talk with me?" Burns says.

"Your neighbor," he consults a piece of paper. "Mister Bricker. Leon Bricker."

"Oh no," Burns says. He thinks about the gun on the counter, the boxes full of god knows what that he and Leon were moving up from the basement yesterday.

The cop pulls out a walkie talkie, says "We have Burns here if you still want to try that." He opens the door for Burns, "Come right this way, sir," he says. "We'll make sure the boy gets back to the house safely."

A young officer kneels down, introduces himself to Tyler. The two shake hands and Burns almost bursts into tears again. Burns leans down to hug Tyler, sees the concern on the boy's face. "I'll be fine," Burns says. "I just need to talk with Mr. Leon for a second and then I'll be home."

He follows the officer through a phalanx of police and fire trucks. The entire place is aglow. All the neighbors are out in front of their houses. Some have drinks, snacks. Most are talking on cell phones or recording the proceedings with various devices, screens held in front of their faces like tiny shields. It is surreal, like a movie set: it is like his neighborhood, his boring little neighborhood of quiet desperation and Costco boxes and little backyard gardens, of baby showers and graduation parties, patio furniture and all wheel drive. It is like that, but illuminated, pulsing with siren-light. Crackling with radios. Sodden with the white noise of news helicopters overhead.

He's led through a series of checkpoints and over to where a group of men are standing behind a police van. "This is him," the officer says.

A short, pudgy man shakes his hand. "Sargeant Strock," he says. "What can you tell us about your neighbor?"

Burns is still in shock. He feels like he's swimming, dreaming. How can this be happening? What is happening? "He's a guitar player. Guitar teacher," Burns says. "I don't think he's, I mean, he never showed any signs before of being, you know, dangerous."

"Where have you been tonight, sir?" Strock says.

"I went to a, um, concert," Burns says. Somehow even in the midst of all this he can't quite bring himself to say Justin Bieber's name, not in front of these guys and their guns, their hooded eyes and the things they've seen, the fact that this—standing in the street at midnight behind a SWAT truck, is their actual job.

"Concert?" Strock says. "Did you have any idea what your neighbor was up to tonight? What he had planned? I mean pre-meditated?"

Burns flashes on the guns, the young people pot, the beautiful bonfire.

"No," he says. "I mean, what did he do? What do you think he had planned?"

"Took a few shots at the Bank of America people. Foreclosure. We had a black and white along for the ride. Took a few shots at the black and white, too. He hasn't hit anybody yet, just a few tires and his own windows. He's either a lousy shot or a good one, but either way, we gotta read the situation the same: he's taken some shots at our men, is well armed and who knows what else he has in there."

"Can I talk to him?" Burns says.

"He's been asking for you," Strock says. He picks up a megaphone and indicates for Burns to follow. They wind their way through the various police and SWAT and firemen along a bulwark of emergency vehicles and over behind a van. "This is going to be loud," Strock says. "Also, get down, behind the van. Sometimes this is when they fire." Burns kneels behind the van. "Mr. Bricker," Strock says. "We have Burns here. He'd like to talk with you."

"Can I go in there?" Burns says.

"Sir," Strock says, and the way he says it, Burns knows he is fed up with people like Burns, desk people who spend their days driving around giving samples to doctors, having meetings, publicly urinating and attending Justin Bieber concerts.

"Sir?" Strock says. He proffers the megaphone. "Quiet!" Strock shouts.

"Leon," Burns says, his voice shoots out over the neighborhood. "It's me. Burns."

"Jesus Christ I know who it is, man!" Leon says. Pussification of America, Burns thinks. Another check in another column. "I need to talk to you, Burns," Leon says. "Come on up here."

Strock shakes his head.

"They won't let me," Burns says.

"Yes they will. Let him up here, Strock," Leon says. "I'm not gonna do anything to him. He's got a kid on the way, for god's sake. He's harmless. I just want to tell him something and then this will all be over."

Strock looks at Burns. It is the same look, Burns thinks, that Leon has given him a million times. The pussification of America. "I'll be fine," Burns says.

The old sergeant sighs, hands Burns a flak jacket. "Put this on," he says. "And I'm going with you."

"We're coming," Strock says into the bullhorn.

"About fucking time," Leon shouts from the house.

Behind them, a row of police with guns is focused in Leon's direction. All is quiet except the hum of engines, the crackle of police radios. As they get closer, Burns can hear another sound, music, drifting in from Leon's house. "Bell Bottom Blues." The original Derek and the Dominoes version. Eric Clapton and Duane Allman on guitar. Something ticks in the back of Burns' mind. Had they had this conversation? He remembers the bonfire – those bills and invoices and advance warnings blazing into oblivion while he and Leon knocked back the bottle of Makers – remembers Leon rhapsodizing about "Layla," about "Bell Bottom Blues," the sublime combination of Allman and Clapton and how there would never be anything like it again. He remembers that things got pretty serious for a while.

"That's close enough," Leon says, and the two men stop in their tracks. Leon peeks his head around the door and there's a quick rustle behind them, rifles locked into place. For the first time, Burns realizes that there's a chance that this is it, that one of these kids-how old are they? Twenty-two? Twenty-five?—will snap and blow his head off. When he's thought of this possibility—death in a car accident, a heart attack, going to sleep and never waking up—it's been a mix of terror and relief. No more Visa bill. No more doctor's offices or traffic, taxes or underarm deodorant or groceries or disappointments. No more disappointing. But now all he can think about is Tyler, Rachel, the unborn baby. The baby. He remembers Tyler, a colicky infant, premature and screaming, every cell in his body wholly unhappy about being out in the world of sunshine and cold, of smells and tastes and big hairy things. Suddenly, that baby smell is ripe is his nose. So clean and full that it takes his breath away and he stops there on the sidewalk. He can feel the thing in his hands—tiny, almost weightless, completely helpless. "Jesus Christ, Burns, what the fuck are you doing?" Leon says. The house is boarded up, dark, and Leon's voice comes through the mail slot. Burns wonders what kind of training Montgomery County police receive, what kind of life insurance the company has on him, if Rachel will still get the settlement if Julie has already submitted the paperwork to have him terminated.

"Let me talk to him a minute," Leon says.

Strock releases his grip and Burns walks to the door. Leon takes a step outside, a shotgun pointed at the ground. He smiles. "Well, amigo," he says. "This is probably it." He runs a hand through sweaty hair. He hasn't shaved in weeks. He looks more than ever like an extra on a Western, the ranch-hand who pulls out a guitar and sings around the campfire.

"Just go with them," Burns says. "Go with them. It will be okay. You're not that old, Leon. You can still..." He stops, unsure of what Leon can still do. Teach guitar in prison is the most likely option. Until he dies. Leon is seventy years old and fired shots at an officer of the law. Maybe worse, at an officer of the bank. The math doesn't work for Leon anymore.

"Figured it out, didn't you?" Leon says. "Finally, he gets it."

"Leon, I'm sorry," Burns says. He feels a pang of grief, swallows a sob because he has to, because now isn't the time to be crying like a nine year old. "Goddamit, Leon," he says. "I saw the most amazing thing tonight."

"That concert," Leon says. "That little kid concert?"

"Yeah," Burns says. "The little kid concert. I think you would have liked it."

"Jesus Christ," Leon says. "Everything is getting worse. All the time."

"I don't think so," Burns says. "Not anymore."

"Gentlemen!" An amplified voice, a megaphone. Burns turns around. Strock has retreated to the police line, is standing behind a cruiser. "Come on down here, the both of you. It's time to wrap this up."

Burns shakes. "Thanks, Leon," he says.

"One more thing," Leon says. "Reason I wanted to talk to you. The guitars are in their cases in the basement. They're for you. For Tyler."

"I—" Burns starts.

"Save it," Leon says. "Take care of them. Tyler and the new one. Take care of them."

Burns nods. He puts a hand on Leon's shoulder. "I'd hug you if it wasn't such a symptom of the pussification of America," he says.

"Men shouldn't hug," Leon says.

"Okay then."

"Okay then. It's time for this to end. Go home."

Burns turns and walks toward the police line. The entire neighborhood is glowing, pulsing with red and blue light. He counts one, two, three...twelve guns aimed at Leon's house, at Burns himself, as he makes his way to Strock. By the time he gets there, he's got the vest off and he drops it on the cruiser.

"Hey!" Strock shouts. "Burns! Burns!"

He makes his way past the police cruisers and the vans and the SWAT vehicle, through his neighbors, huddled in bunches, holding beers and coffee mugs. In the distance, he hears a shout and then the firecracker *ratatat* of twelve guns. It lasts for a few seconds and then it's over. Burns pauses. "Shit, Leon," he says. He keeps on walking.

There is a light on in his house. He can see the glow of the television. Rachel stands at the window. She holds a hand up to the glass. The baby will be here soon. Burns wonders what a four bedroom two bath would go for in Scranton. It's not too late. He knows that now. He puts his head down and makes his way home.

What It Means to Be

Tom Williams

For Carmen and Finn

"Why doesn't Daddy talk about when he was a little boy?"

Don't look so surprised, James! You've known this question was coming. You've known it since the day he was born. Your son. The Buddy. The present occupant of the car seat in the back of your CRV (the safe and economic choice in SUVs). The present sleeping occupant of the seat, trained, it seems, since a bout with colic at seven months, to fall asleep precisely when a vehicle has been in motion for forty minutes. Measuring fifty-two inches, weighing forty-eight and a half pounds, he's more a lookalike of his mother, but whenever you gaze upon him, you know he's yours, 100 percent your boy.

Only he's not asking the question. The interlocutor sits beside you, Amy, your wife of only six months longer than your son's five years on earth—oops!—and she says the question again in case you weren't listening or pretending you couldn't hear. She knows all your tricks. No need to try and avoid this line or ask her to repeat herself while you scramble for time. She pats her hair—cut short for summer—takes off her sunglasses and stares until you turn her way.

"He's right, you know. You never talk about what you were like when you were his age. You never talk about what you were like at any age." She clears her throat, softens her eyes. Her touch surprises and comforts at once. "Why not?"

You wish there were a simple answer. You wish there were a single answer. Some punchy remark that could fit on a TV screen like those you craft easily for your clients. But there's either so much to say or the answer is simple but nothing you want to share. Right now, you're not ready to decide. You've got a task ahead of you: managing the remaining miles from Louisville, your home of the last two years, to Chicagoland, where your dad, the proudest granddad of the Midwest, awaits. A Friday in June, with Father's Day mere hours away, and the terrain you're traveling is all you can focus on for now.

"I'm just letting you know," your wife says. Sunglasses back on, she rests her head against the seat as if she might join her son in slumber. "You might want to start thinking about an answer."

You say, "It's not just" and then whatever remaining words you have slip through the space between the window and the door frame. That Amy is allowing you to haul her up to see your dad instead of a trip to see hers in Cincinnati is reason enough for you to provide her more than a fragment. Further, she's got terrible allergies, and your dad won't get rid of the cat your mother brought into the house two years before she died. But you've got shitty drivers and waning light to contend with. That's right, James. If you don't focus all your efforts on passing these two pickups, the whole trip might fall apart. That's what forces your silence. That's what sets the grim look upon your face.

Amy says, "Think about it. He wants to know who you are."

Of course he does, you want to say but instead put more weight on the accelerator, as if this moment's a marker you can pass and never see again.

This is what you know about yourself: you've achieved far more than you ever dreamed. Only a few years ago you discovered the things that used to own you—drink, drugs and other vices—no longer needed to run your life ragged. You managed to clean up, walk straight, keep a job longer than two years, cultivate a talent to tell clients what they could do to get customers to say yes to the goods and services provided. You and biology, it seems, found a woman who wanted to stay on a path that meant something. More self-improvement remains, of course. You need to bring your advertising firm up from the four-man crew it is currently to an honest-to-goodness company with receptionists and plants and pastel prints. You need to minimize the number of cigarettes that need to be smoked before you quit. You need to quit flirting. You need to take care of your dad, a widower after your mother's heart attack. And all these things you can envision yourself doing as clearly as if they are presented on the HDTV you installed in the living room two weeks ago with only a modicum of cursing. Yet one thing you can't envision is what your wife and son are asking for: you and the Buddy engaged in a discussion of the life you endured before things got better. And why, James? Because you worry that to share your story with your son might activate in him some dormant gene that will steer him toward the pitfalls you couldn't avoid and from which perhaps only dumb luck saved you? That pattern might not repeat itself with the Buddy. He might not be as lucky. In short: you don't want him to be you.

At your boyhood home, your dad is standing in the doorway, knowing without Facebook or a smartphone the exact moment of your arrival. He hugs Amy first, and after you hand over a still groggy grandson, your dad embraces the Buddy. Once upon a time, you expected him to slam doors in your face, but it's different now, not just because of your mother's death but because you're finally comfortable with what it means to be you—the son of a black father and white mother as well as an alcoholic and an addict—and you no longer resent him for bringing you into the world. You're not here to borrow money any more, or hole up until you can find whatever's needed to re-enter the world. You're here because you want to be. You're here because you have seen what your own dad's life must have been like years ago when you were the Buddy's age. Well, kind of. And you're here this weekend to celebrate, both of you as fathers deserving honor and feting on what is a dubious holiday, no doubt maintained by bigger ad firms to keep their greeting card and golf course clients happy. You turn to retrieve the luggage, tell your dad you don't need his help, which prompts him to toss the Buddy in the air—he's still as strong as he was when you left—and then lead him and Amy inside.

Dragging your bags behind you, you open the screen door with your foot. Every house is chockablock with stuff, photo albums, tchotchkes, old clothes and shoeboxes. Two weeks ago, your dad hired an estate sale agency to clear out the possessions of your mom's he'll let go, an important step. But aside from the clutter, the vacuum tracks in the carpet promise a thorough, professional cleaning. Still, there it is, you can tell, the lingering odor of cat. And you can't tell your dad to get rid of the cat or tell Amy to dope up on Benadryl. Plus, the Buddy loves the old tabby, who answers to both Boo and Bob and sleeps every night by your dad's feet. A night in a hotel still might be best for Amy. You might even leave after Sunday's Father's Day Lunch instead of Monday morning. You need to get back to plan a presentation for a family-owned maker of snack cakes. Amy stands in the middle of the foyer, watching you struggle with the luggage, then points to where your dad and Buddy are fondling brand new racing cars before setting them on a black oval track. An old urge to ask where was that when you were a kid comes up, but you'd rather smile and wrap your arm around your wife. She's a foot shorter than you but a strength both physical and emotional radiates. She steps out of your embrace.

"Where's the cat?" she says, then yawns.

Among the tottering books and dresses, coats, umbrellas and picture frames stacked here and there in the living room, dining room and kitchen, there appear any number of places to hide, but Boo or Bob cannot be found. The Hot Wheels racing seems to have slowed too, and when you look at the Buddy again, he's yawning. He folds his arms, then lays his head atop them.

"I think someone needs to go to bed," Amy says. The Buddy tries to lift his arms off the floor, as if he can't get his head to move on its own, but his is the next weight in your arms as you take him upstairs. Not to your room, it turns out, but to the guest bedroom, where the single bed's made and there's a trophy and plaques your dad won as an all-state linebacker. Lately, Buddy has said he we wants to play but all the concussion talk, from Pop Warner to the Pro Bowl, worries you. Or maybe you envy that your dad's skill skipped you and landed in the sleepy limbs you lay on the bed. After his clothes are off and he's covered by a blanket, you pass Amy on her way to your old room. She's not sneezing yet, but she's swallowing a couple of tablets and not offering you more than a good night as she opens the door.

Downstairs, in the kitchen, your dad has two glasses waiting and a bottle of your old favorite, Beam, on the breakfast bar. Next to the bottle sits a deck of cards. Where, you wonder, is the computer you bought him last Father's Day to play Solitaire and send email? Before he starts pouring—and he's always had a shot and a half pour—you select one of the glasses, fill it with water. He says, "I always forget. I'm sorry. It's all right if I have one, though, right?"

"Go ahead, Dad." It's only been the last few years you called him that, even in your head, instead of "him" or "he" or an icy "father." And you're not going to begrudge him ten drinks if that's what he needs now.

You sit down next to him. The breakfast bar once witnessed some of the most silent meals in Christendom. Now you clutch his empty hand.

"It's good to be here," you say.

Your glasses clink. He downs his glass, refills it. You sip the water instead of gulping it. Your dad says, "You ever get tempted now and then?" He's sipping now, and instantly you recall his warnings about not drinking too heavily around upper management types, always white, always ready to find fault in their minority wards.

"Every day," you say, because it's true. Even when you're thirsty, like now, you avoid any motion like chugging so it doesn't trigger thoughts that haven't disappeared just yet, even after eight years. You shrug. "I just tell myself this isn't the right time for it." You pause, roll your empty glass between your palms. "Used to be every day was the right time for it." But that's not why you're here, is it, James, to rehash your bad days or revel in your sobriety. You fill up your glass with water for another toast. "Happy Father's Day," you say.

"Same to you," your dad says.

"Strange to hear that, to be honest."

"It's still early. Five years in, Jimmy."

That name—that no one else calls you, now that that your mother is gone—seems as lovingly expressed as a poem. Your hand is again on his before you know it. "Learned everything I know from you." As your dad looks at you, you recall the vain wish that somehow fatherhood would allow you to resemble your progenitor more, yet without a mirror you can see that, if anything, you now look even more like your mother's father than before: blue eyes and an underbite in a long face the color of pancake batter. Your dad's thumb rubs your knuckles, still a few shades darker but in it you feel the same strength you felt trying to arm-wrestle your dad. His record with you is undefeated, whereas with the Buddy you've not even tried. Who doesn't want to initiate: him or you? Your dad yawns. You don't want to lose this chance. You tell him, "The Buddy wonders why I don't talk about my childhood."

"I'm not surprised." Your dad pauses, finishes the rest of his drink. "It's karma, Jimmy."

"I asked you to tell me about your childhood?"

"No, you didn't ask me about anything. Besides, you weren't exactly a great listener."

Whether this is karma or not isn't the point. You do know many of your dad's stories, could talk of his exploits growing up without a father of his own, the brooms his mother broke on his head, the South Side streets he ran with his friends and their impossible names: Bullet, Pork Chop, Night Train and Smoke. Yet these are just details—difficult to forget. What do you know about your dad as a young man, James? Were you listening to him then? Are you now? You say, "It's just, you know, sometimes I feel like I know what I'm doing at work. Other times I feel like I'm a decent husband. And then I feel like I'm not the worst father in the world."

Out of nowhere, the cat leaps on your dad's lap. It rubs his face against his hand as if it can't get enough. Your dad nods. He opens his eyes and you say, "But I can't be good at all three at once, and I might be sacrificing being a dad to keep the other two things going." That's not all you want to say—there's that other detail you just can't seem to share with another; you might not even be able to expose it fully to yourself. But your father is pursing his lips and savoring, it seems, the last of the Beam. He says, "You just don't think you can have everything going right at the same time?"

"Yes," you say, as relieved as one to whom a sage has stated the mysteries of existence.

"You think that's possible?"

"I hope so?" Suddenly, a sip of Beam seems even more tempting. Would it open a channel in your mind to the let the words out that the Buddy wants to hear?

Your dad laughs, uncaps the bottle for one last splash of bourbon. The cat stays on his lap, purring. You say, "Did you ever think you had everything together?"

"Yep." He licks his lips, drains the glass and sets it down, grinning but silent. He knows the joke but won't reveal until you ask. His dark hands now glide over the cat's white fur. Do you tell him now that he looks like the villain in a James Bond movie—movies you didn't watch together when you were both younger, so much younger? No, you opt for a question.

"And then what happened?"

"You were born, Jimmy."

The next morning, you're the last out of bed, engulfed by the warmth of a mattress you're pretty sure is the same one you slept on throughout high school. Is it older than your wife? Probably. Downstairs, the Buddy is amped as he always is on a Saturday, intrigued by the different cartoons this cable TV gets and impressed by the breakfast your dad has prepared: scratch biscuits, scrambled eggs, sausages in link and patty, and enough bacon to make you wonder if your dad's been hoarding. Amy's impressed too, already spooning eggs onto a biscuit and topping it with an X of bacon and a square of American cheese. Through the mouthful she munches, she says it's her second and encourages you to join everyone.

"Never ate breakfast when he was little," your dad says. "Liked coffee with milk and sugar since he was ten but never started eating until around noon." As if in evidence, a mug of coffee is in your hand, but you remember differently: it wasn't the food you were trying to avoid back then, it was the man who made it. But, as if to show there's no hard feelings, or that he's nowhere near the truth, you sit next to Amy at the breakfast bar and pile your plate with eggs and links. The lightness and flavor of the eggs is familiar, but you first acquaint this with your granny, your dad's mother. Have his eggs always been this good? Is he making these kinds of breakfast all the time now or is this just for the occasion of you and your small family—you and the Buddy are his only blood relatives alive—and your visit? Does it matter, James? Amy's always instructing you to live more in the moment. You dig in.

By the time you finish, everyone else's plates are soaking in sudsy water in the sink, and your dad and the Buddy are headed outside, purportedly in search of Boo/Bob but perhaps giving you some time alone with Amy. You check in, inquire about the state of her sinuses, and she reports they're okay, for the most part, but an occasional sneeze sounds foreboding. She pops four more Benadryls, asks you what you talked about with your dad the night before. You swig more coffee, say that he seems in good spirits, fine health, and that you can't believe how well you all get along these days. "Did you tell him about what the Buddy asked?" she says.

You nod, say, "He told me it was karma. Said I never listened."

Amy's laughter sounds more sharp than caressing. It's not meant to bring you in closer but to let you know she agrees, which she makes clear when she says, "Well, you're consistent."

"Consistent how?"

At least her fingers are warm and soft against your face. Her laughter still hasn't ceased and she's shaking her head as she does when her freshmen can't master the simplest of skills. "He's right, your dad. You don't listen, especially when it's stuff you don't want to hear."

In your head, a number of clients' faces pass by, reaching the teens, the twenties. All of them, repeat customers now, have said at least once how what separated you and your firm from all the rest in Louisville was how well you listened. One, a bourbon magnate, who would later confirm that he and his family had never had dealings with a—quote-unquote—minority-owned firm before, assured you and your staff that no others made him feel more secure. "It's like y'all know what I'm going to say before I even speak a word," he claimed.

But that's work. That's different. When Amy stops laughing you lean back in your seat, say, "I heard what you said, what the Buddy asked you."

"And what are you going to do about that? What's your plan?"

Amy stands, heads back to the breakfast bar for a few more bites of bacon. Your eyes drift toward the picture window behind the TV. Ambling past is the Buddy, your dad a few steps behind, their attention arrested by something out of your view. Your dad's lips are moving but it's too distant to know what he says. You turn back to Amy, who at least is still smiling. "I don't want him to end up like me," you say. There, it's said. At least one secret you've been keeping close to your vest.

A sharp ruffling sound reaches your ears. You turn and see Amy flipping her thumb against the corner of your dad's deck of cards. "Baby," she says. "Not talking to him isn't going to keep him on the right path."

The image in your mind now is the Queen of Hearts in *The Manchurian Candidate*—the original with Sinatra, not that train wreck with Denzel: the display of the card forcing poor

Laurence Harvey to do things the sensible part of him would never imagine. Only, in your version, it's your words somehow awakening in the Buddy's very DNA the snoozing bad habits that possessed and plagued you for so long, ushering him into an all too similar set of circumstances.

If you squint, you can see the physical features of your own face and body in his but the passersby in grocery stores and airports always talk about how much he favors his mother. Who's to say he's going to be anything like you, James? Maybe he's his own person. Maybe he can take what you give him and leave the rest behind. Maybe he's not doomed. Open your eyes. Look at your wife. She's still riffling her thumb against the cards. She needs you to say you'll try. And after you do walk over and say this, she embraces you, in time to hear the front door slap open, the Buddy run in with Boo/Bob in both arms.

"Momma," he says. "The kitty!"

Amy's still breathing. Her eyes aren't swollen shut. And meantime, the Buddy and his grandpa race Hot Wheels while the Cubs struggle on the TV. Every now and then, the Buddy's attention will drift. Some object of the many in the room will attract him and he'll have it in his hands and your dad will share its history. That photo is of grandpa's grandpa, a bootblack and butter and egg man in Maysville, Kentucky. That clamshell came from the first beach he ever visited. That empty bank in the shape of a *Model T* was your Granny's and once it contained enough spare change to pay for a bicycle that she rode in her last years.

Though you've seen all these objects, held them in your hands (Weren't you the five-year-old who picked up the shell from that cold stretch of Cape Cod sand?), they seem to you now as foreign as Farsi. Still, you're appreciative of how this gives you more time with Amy, even though she seems more engaged in witnessing what's going on than paying attention to you. She offers up her bare feet to the pressure of your thumbs but keeps watching as your dad leads the Buddy over to the kitchen—could it be time for lunch already? He's saying, "I tried to teach your dad once. He always was too busy by himself in his room."

All too true, you silently admit, though you don't need Amy saying, "And he's still up in his room by himself too much. Or his office."

You start to wonder if your wife and dad are in cahoots somehow. They seem like they've been rehearsing in secret. It was, after all, her idea to come up here, and then it seems as clear as if the words are spoken to you that, even if there was no active conspiracy, things are working out in a way to make it simpler for you to share with the Buddy what you were like as a little boy. Hell, your dad's laying the groundwork for you. Amy's not piling on, she's making the connections between then and now, so the Buddy can see these aren't just events in isolation but pieces of how the you that you are today started in the you you were when you were the Buddy's age. Problem is, you can't shake the feeling that what's really revealed is how slow on the uptake you are. Bad enough that it took you nearly four decades to even become a husband, that you're still figuring out the how of it. Your real work as a son's only a few years longer than the Buddy's been on the planet, and don't even pretend you've got fatherhood figured out. You want to sink into this couch until you disappear or hover like a spirit over your dad and son, learning just how to be better at both roles. Question is, do you have time to observe or do you need to act? This weekend's still open. You might leave Sunday afternoon or wait until Monday morning. But you haven't even decided the time is right to confront your past with the Buddy. It seems the two real adults in the room have done that for you, and, like a child, you want to resist, show them that theirs isn't the only way. Still, it seems time to at least get off the couch.

Amy harumphs disappointment that you're not rubbing her feet any more, and she follows you as you walk to the kitchen, where at the breakfast bar, the Buddy is struggling to shuffle the deck of cards. He can cut them into stacks but the cards are too stiff for him to shuffle. You wait for two more tries before you move in and show off. You tap the two stacks together, perform two one-handed cuts. The first is shaky but the second brings a smile to the Buddy's face. Goddamn, he looks like his momma, doesn't he, James, those dimples and even white teeth. Next, you warm up with a couple of shuffles, show off with a rainbow bridge and go back to one-handed cuts when the Buddy claps and laughs. You smack down the deck on the breakfast bar, wink. But before you can enjoy this status as something other than the dad who is apparently not around enough or talkative enough, your dad sits down next to the Buddy, and after only a few cuts and shuffles, he says, "Have I ever told you the story of . . ."

"Little Joe," you finish for him. Jesus Christ, Jimmy, you've used those two words over and over in the years since you left this house vowing never to return, but not in combination, and not to describe the card trick that's happening right now. You need to sit down and do.

"That's right. The story of Little Joe," your dad says. "I haven't done this since your dad was a boy."

When he lays down the six of spades, you know there is no longer any question who the real father in this house is. Whether the visit was designed for this purpose doesn't matter. You will not have anything to say that would impress or encourage your son to learn more about you. It's all about grandpa now, who miraculously walks the Buddy through this trick, its four kings that appear one after another, *thwap, thwap, thwap, thwap,* followed by the four queens, and the four jacks joining them soon after, Little Joe always popping up despite cuts and taps and all manner of ruses that you can't even discover for yourself. You feel your wife's breath on your neck as she leans closer. Her smile betrays, perhaps, an attraction to your dad, and who can blame her. She knows too when there is a real man around. So when your dad is about to lay down the four aces, he says, "And there was the ace booze." He shoots you a look, the same concern on his face as last night with the bottle of Beam, but you shake your head. Go on. It's all right, Dad. No one bothers to explain what booze is to the Buddy, because who needs to? He's staring at your dad's hands as if he's shaping existence and history out of these cards, injecting personality and life into these pieces of paper. It's not difficult to imagine yourself in the same position as the Buddy, though you suspect you were older when you first started to see Little Joe. More than anything, you're trying to recall the secret to the trick. Once your dad showed you. When was that? Whenever it was, you don't know how to cut and shuffle to and keep the story going, the cards appearing as if by, what other word suffices, magic. And it seems right now you're in three places at once: watching your dad and the Buddy, recalling the first time you saw the trick and the time you stopped paying attention because your dad did this all the time and embarrassed you. But when you feel your shoulder dampen and recognize that the source is Amy's sneezes, four or five in a row, you turn and see that the Benadryl aren't working and what she's saying is that more pills won't help. You've got one arm around her as she sneezes some more. The Buddy says, "Momma" and your dad's on the phone for a moment, then right by Amy's side and saying that, just in case this happened, he'd called a pal over at the Holiday Inn nearby. "I'm not going to d-i-e," she says, because the Buddy knows way too much about d-e-a-t-h, what with your mother last year and Amy's grandparents, one in December, the other in March, and a classmate in preschool just weeks ago. But she does need to get out of this house and your dad's got his keys and he's saying he can come back and get her stuff, which leaves you and the Buddy standing still. Has the universe interceded to give you time alone with the Buddy in your dad's house? When the front door shuts and you turn to the Buddy, you see him looking at the six of spades, Little Joe himself, as though he might uncover the secret to the sleight of hand his granddad just performed. You look back to the front door and neither your wife nor your dad is coming back in to say surprise and that's definitely your dad's Buick headed out of the drive. It's just the two of you, and the Buddy won't take his eyes off the cards until you clear your throat. You sit down. He sets down the six of spades and says, "Do you know how to do this?"

For a moment it's in you to fake it, but you needed to have listened better to your dad when you were younger to even approximate the crudest duplication now. So you shake your head and watch the Buddy's bottom lip droop. Grandpa didn't even get a chance to finish the story of Little Joe. But perhaps you could use this moment, James. Perhaps you could build upon what your dad and wife have done to assure the Buddy that you don't mind talking about yourself as a little boy, that you're willing to share. Yet the words, the words, they won't come. Is it shame? Is it fear? Is it just that you've not heard yourself talking about your life in any way that makes sense?

Whatever the case, the Buddy has moved on. The moment is over. With both hands he stirs the cards together and keeps stirring until the cards spread out and a few spill off the edge of the breakfast bar. The Buddy doesn't bother to clean up his mess. He's off the stool and headed to the TV and his new Hot Wheels track. All you can do is watch.

A half hour under the spray of a hot shower and some time alone in the Holiday Inn, and Amy's restored enough to enjoy supper out with you, the Buddy and grandpa. After the chicken wings are finished but before the burgers arrive, she makes it clear that she can't spend any more time in the house this weekend. A pair of questions remains: how much longer should you stay up here in Chicagoland, and where should the Buddy sleep tonight.

According to your dad, she can have the room for one night or two—either way, it's on him, as he's apologetic for not vacuuming every microbe of cat dander in the house. Amy's nonchalant. In fact, she seem still flirty with your dad, praising him for his foresight to have the room reserved, acknowledging again that there's clearly one real man around. You don't mind what happens, just as long as you know in advance, which leaves the decision up to the Buddy, who makes it clear by hugging grandpa and saying, "Can we stay in your house?" What's left then in the meal is the two sundaes and three spoons (none for you, thanks) and a tussle over the check that you actually win. Then it's time to drop Amy back at her room. She waves and enters, and you're not sure, but she seems happier about more than avoiding allergens. Maybe she's happy to spend time away from you.

That's the wrong kind of thinking, James. It never serves you well. Focus on the moment, your dad driving you around in his roomy Buick over the same roads where you learned how to drive. Yet twenty years ago there was farmland, there was space, there wasn't some car lot or big box store or fast food franchise on every quarter acre of land. The landscape of your youth is no more, which feels like a fairly weighty thought. Childhood exists only in your memory, yet you don't want to, what, open that door, turn to that page, what? Those snack food makers in Hendersonville might benefit from this line of thought. Since nobody wants to eat refined sugar and processed flour anymore, out of fear of all the cholesterol and calories, the only seduction left is some nostalgic impulse. Yet isn't this just the kind of thing that Amy would detect, were she here: you not being in the moment with the Buddy, you losing another chance to let him into some understanding that though you believe your life truly began the day you got sober, there was some life that led you there first? Check on him. He's awake and you're too close to your dad's house for him to sleep. What does he see out his window? It looks just like the area you live in now, just like any American suburb, the only difference is the temperature. The Buddy says, "Grandpa, can we do Little Joe again?"

"If it's all right with your daddy."

For a moment, you don't think that term applies to you. But you nod, then say, "It's okay with me," and you're on your way back home.

"You were right last night," you say to your dad after the Buddy's gone to sleep.

Your dad taps together the playing cards—Little Joe should be weary after all the times he gathered his friends, ladies, Jack brothers and the ace booze—says, "Right about what?"

"I didn't listen," you say. "As a kid."

There's no Beam out tonight, which is probably for the best. You might not find what's needed to resist. "That's just it, Jimmy," your dad says. "You were a kid. All's forgiven" He shuffles the cards, deals out a hand of solitaire. Where's that computer, you want to ask again, but watch as he sets up his orderly rows, always sure to keep the cards from overlapping, his sequences as well laid out as his stories or his account of Little Joe's doings. You say, "Little Joe—you taught me once. I have no idea how to do it now." You pause, think to yourself that red five goes on black six just as your dad pairs those cards. It feels foolish to even allow the thought, but it's here, it's near, you may as well say it: "I feel somehow that if I'd listened better, I wouldn't have ended up the drunk I was before I met Amy and had the Buddy."

Chuckling, your dad looks up from the cards. How white his hair's gotten. His face, still smooth, makes him resemble even more his mother, who didn't see sixty. He says, "You can't change what already has happened." He places a black queen on a red king, which uncovers an ace of spades to place close to the sugar bowl. "Besides, a wise man once told me that sometimes, in order to have the good times, you have to endure some of the shit." He smiles, drags his front teeth over his bottom lip. "That was you, Jimmy."

"You pay attention," you say. "You're a good listener."

"You know who's also a good listener?" Your dad points his chin upward, in the direction of where the Buddy is now sleeping. What does he dream about? Goddam, James, you need to ask him. Your dad says, "When you were paying the check, he asked me where Smoke and Bullit were now."

"You were talking about those guys? Where are they now?"

"Dead."

"Of course."

This news—if you can even call it that—strikes with far more force than it should. You never met either of these men, can only summon the barest descriptions from your dad's stories, and yet you're blinking and the inside of your nose tingles from imminent tears. You didn't think you'd cry at your mother's funeral—there was a time you secretly feared she'd be at yours—but once you started, the tears seemed to have no beginning or ending, as if they might never cease. You shake your head now, while your dad turns more cards, manages a few more moves but fails to complete the game. A long breath issues from his nose as he taps together the cards again, then places them between you. "Point is," your dad says, "he wants to hear about what you were like. You don't have to tell him every single thing you did."

"I don't even know where to start."

"Doesn't matter." He picks up the cards, tosses one to you, one to him, until you've both got five. "How many?"

You assume it's five card draw you're playing, and snatch up your hand to see nothing but low numbers. Where are all those face cards now? With a three, a four and a six, you ask for two, knowing the unlikelihood of the straight before you get a ten and a nine of diamonds.

"Two for the dealer," your dad says. His heart flush is no surprise, but what he says following it is: "Sometimes, you just start dealing what you've got. Hope for the best."

The morning brings a call from Amy and the clarification that she is in no way ready to check out by noon, so it's best that you all plan to leave on Monday morning. She wants you to know as well that you should be using this opportunity to talk to the Buddy, and while she doesn't admit to any conspiracy with your dad, she states clearly that what you should be doing is following your dad's lead and just tell stories. That's what your son wants to hear. You don't tell her that after trying, before you fell asleep, to recall anything you might say about the first thirty-some years of your life, that you believe you don't have any stories, just discreet incidents of humiliation, fear, self-loathing and pain. You tell Amy you'll try and she says the free breakfast at the Holiday Inn doesn't rival what your dad put together just the day before. "You ought to cook breakfast more often," she says. "Be more like your dad." Silently, you concede that's probably always been the case, then head downstairs, the last one out of bed again.

Fortunately or unfortunately, the morning's consumed with breakfast and talking about what to do for the rest of the day. You also find the computer you got for your dad on his desk in the living room under a pile of laundered shirts with the year-old receipt on top. You email one of your partners, Terry, that you won't be back in the office until Tuesday. You append in the email your thought for the snack cake company about childhood returning with a bite of their fried pie. As a gesture to Amy, you don't even respond to his reply that arrives before you can exit your account. In the family room, Buddy can't get enough of the cat, and it comes running whether the Buddy calls it Boo or Bob. It seems like no time has passed at all since your first coffee and when you're piled in the Buick to pick up Amy for a Father's Day brunch at, your dad's choice, the Jade Garden, a Chinese restaurant where the red and gold dragon and lantern decor hasn't changed since the decade you all moved here. The menu looks unchanged, its entrees engineered to put people at ease and allow them to recognize that it's chicken, pork and beef they're eating and not any household pet that someone's come to love. Before the Anglo waitress takes your order, gifts and cards are given, and your dad is happy with his Amex gift card, as he's sure there's no point in acquiring more things, what with him trying to clean out what he already has. Right now it feels like all you need is the signature on the card with Lightnin' McQueen that approximates the Buddy's name, but you don't mind the gift certificate for Men's Wearhouse either. As a matter of fact, you've got something 44-regular in khaki in mind.

Staring at the menu, you're pretty sure both your mom and your dad would eat the pork foo young more often than not, so that's what you ask for, and you look around at the other folk assembled here, all of them looking as they should: American families celebrating their fathers. You know that this was a place you ate often because the owners would never tell the wait staff to not serve you and your parents or ask you three to leave to avoid upsetting the other diners. In fact, as you survey the room you see some other families with mothers and fathers of different races and their children of varying beige hues, a stark indication that the world the Buddy has entered will be much simpler for him to navigate than was yours and, for certain, your dad's. Yet that doesn't convince you harmony in all things awaits him. In fact, you know that he has an even harder story to tell, what with, "My mom's white, my dad's biracial, my dad's nearly ten years older than my mom. Oh yeah, and a recovering alcoholic." But look, James, there is your dad, holding up a glass of water and saying, "I know it's a happy Father's Day for both of us." It seems there's more, but he pauses, and the sudden tightness of your dad's face tells you he doesn't want to cry. He says, "But I can't help looking around and thinking that someone's missing."

The Buddy studies the Chinese zodiac placemat. After all, he was born in the Year of the Monkey. But Amy pats your dad's hand that rests near his own paper placemat and you say through a closing throat, "There is." And though you know it's your mother he's referring to, you can't help but claim that emptiness as yours, that these three have figured out a way to be together and you're still hovering around, waiting for the right opportunity instead of—what did your dad say the night before?—just dealing and discovering what comes out. Thank god the kitchen's efficient and your orders simple, for when the sliver topped dishes come out and they're placed, family style, in the center of the table, the aroma's enough to get everyone focused on eating again. Your dad says thank you and holds your hand for an instant, but you're looking at the Buddy, who can't break his chopsticks open but can spear a hunk of sweet and sour pork with the ends.

Thank god, too, the food is amazing. You've dined, often on a client's tab, at Szechuan and Pacific Rim and Fusion places in Seattle, Houston, the Chinatowns of Manhattan and San Fran, yet the humble productions of this kitchen occupy everyone so much that the only sound is chewing and assenting how good it is. You feel you never want to eat anything else again. The gravy of the egg foo young may have never been served to an actual person of Chinese descent but what does that kind of authenticity matter now? To taste a recipe which was probably only a decade old when your parents were first eating it, these many years later? What more could you ask for? Even when the check arrives, you're so blissed-out on MSG that you don't fight your dad for who pays. For much of the weekend, he's been everyone's father. Why stop now?

The departure plan is still to leave on Monday morning but for you and the Buddy to sleep in the Holiday Inn with Amy after the Buddy's had some more hours with grandpa. You and Amy are hoping he might fall asleep in the CRV on the ride to the hotel from your dad's place, especially if he devotes as much energy as he has been to spending every moment as close to your dad as a shadow. The memory of Amy's last kiss is still on your lips. You placed your chin on the top of her head and said you were married to the right woman, you were so lucky to have her in your life. Right before she entered the doors to the Holiday Inn lobby, though, she mouthed the words, "Talk to him."

To do so now would be intrusive. The Buddy and your dad, again at the breakfast bar, work over the steps of the Little Joe trick. As much as you'd like to see for yourself just how the magic is done, you also sense that, as it's going to be some time between this visit and the next (and, don't say it, James, don't say it) and there's no guarantee, really, of that next visit at all. Bob or Boo leaps on the couch and you keep him off your lap but scratch him around the ears, promising Amy from this distance that you'll scrub with Brillo and rubbing alcohol if need be. Your phone keeps alerting you about incoming texts and emails but you don't consult it or your dad's computer. You watch your son. You watch your dad.

There might be jokes about how doting grandparents are also the same people who fucked up their kids, but that seems irrelevant now. What is relevant is how much you can tell, even without looking, just by hearing the excitement in the Buddy's voice, that he is getting it. Your dad is guiding him to an understanding of how to place the cards in such a way as to produce the right results and he is getting it. Occasionally you can hear the cards sputter from his too small hands but your dad guides him back to where he was before that slip up and leads him forward, one step, then the next. The voice you hear is as soothing as you've ever heard from your dad. He never spoke this way to you, but how would you know? You barely heard the words, let alone the way in which he spoke them, what with the distance you tried to put between you. Didn't listen? James, you barely heard. What you can hear now is this:

"That's right. You deal out the four kings. Good job. Then you follow that with a cut. That's right, again. Now how many blocks does he need to walk to pick up the four queens?"

Waking up from a nap's not something you've done in a while. So the surge of alertness and uncertainty as to how long you've been asleep and where you are snaps you off the couch, startling Boo or Bob and making both the Buddy and your dad laugh. Your dad says Amy called and that she wants you and the Buddy to shower before you come to the hotel. The mention of leaving prompts Buddy to pout. He's shuffling cards like a Vegas dealer now, looking at your dad and asking, "Can't we stay one more day?"

"Your dad's got to get back to work," your dad says. And you wish this weren't true, but it's also helpful knowing you've got Terry already transforming your thoughts into Power Points and charts that might impress the clients on Friday. Tuesday might be a half day for you, James. You are the boss, aren't you? Some time soon you need to stay home with the Buddy, or take him to a ball game or out to eat for Chinese. Surely there's some place back home as unconsciously retro as the Jade Palace. Just the two of you. That's what's needed.

For now, though, it's time for you to be, well, dad, and say, "Come on, Buddy. Let's get showered up and headed over to see mommy soon."

He's still looking at your dad, but smiling. "Should I show him?" he says. Now he cuts the cards, shuffles, and makes a bridge.

"I think you've got enough time for one," your dad says, and he gets up from the chair for you to sit next to your son, who is now, clearly, the second best card sharp in your family, as he says, "This is the story of Little Joe," in a voice that sounds remarkably like Christopher Robin's and your dad's. The cards don't always come out perfectly, but the errors are easily overlooked and when things work—the four kings; the Jack brothers—an outpouring of pride brings your hands together and your own praise: "Awesome!" The Buddy shushes you. The trick's not over. When he speaks of the aces, though, he calls them the ace boots, which makes no sense in the context of the story but is far more appropriate for a five year old to say, you suppose, if five year olds are to be showing off any card tricks at all. You glance at your dad, offer a nod of thanks. He winks. And when the Buddy lays down the final card and you both applaud, the bond between him and your dad and you and your dad feels as real as the breakfast bar beneath your hands. The transitive property won't work here, though: you need to make sure today that's it's not forty years down the line when the Buddy is feeling about you the way you feel about your dad, who was twenty-three when you were born, not forty, and didn't spend a solid ten years trying to destroy every good thing in his life he had going for him, health included.

You say, "You go ahead and shower first."

"That way," your dad says as the Buddy stacks the cards. "We can spend some time together just before you go."

He's sprinting upstairs before the words have faded into the void. The water comes on and your son shrieks as he gets in too fast under water too hot for him, so eager to be back down here with his grandpa. You and your dad follow him, into your old bedroom for the last scan for loose socks and change and anything else that belongs in the suitcases for the ride home. Your dad says, "Thank you, Jimmy. What a wonderful Father's Day present."

"You can get yourself what you want this time, instead of a computer for a paperweight."

Your dad hands over some of the Buddy's pajamas. You stuff them in the suitcase. Amy will probably freak over this but you'll blame the time crunch and beg forgiveness. You'll say, "Wanted to get back and see you" and it won't be a total lie. Your dad says, "Not the card." The skin around his eyes puckers as he squeezes shut his eyes. "You know what I mean."

The embrace is sudden, strong. You don't want to let go. That is, until the bathroom door slams and you feel the Buddy's slim body angling between you both. He's still wet, a little soapy around the ears, and holding on to your dad's knees. "My turn," you say.

It takes three tries to get into the CRV. The Buddy just can't let go of his grandpa and you totally understand. When the deck of cards, complete with case, and both jokers, is in his hands, the Buddy allows himself to be buckled into the car seat. Of course, he needs one more kiss from your dad before he allows you to shake hands and promise that the next time won't be so long. In fact, he's got some time—he's got all the time in the world, he says—as soon as he gets the estate sales guys in and finds himself in as empty a house as he can make it. Behind the wheel, you wave, then pilot the CRV down the residential streets, noting how what were once saplings now cast huge shadows over lawns, and that obviously the Monroes haven't been in the Tudor on the corner for years, and that an Indian family now occupies the Bascombes' old split level near the entrance to the development.

There is time. You know this. There is no need to start divulging every incident of your past to your son on this late evening drive of a Sunday in June. Opportunities might arise as near as tomorrow and as distant as your own deathbed, but they will arise. Only you know this isn't one hundred percent true. You have been too long in the business of making people want things—often that they don't need—to know that one of the main understandings that horrify and link us all is that tomorrow is no guarantee. Brake lights flash ahead and you shift your foot from the gas, but traffic moves on. Without rehearsing all the possible tragedies that could befall you, you know one of them could occur, and there is no comfort in oblivion. You clear your throat. A long pour from your dad's bottle of Beam might moisten your throat and unloose all the events in your head, but that's not for you, James. But no use in wishing for a glass of water either. You clear your throat again. "You're going to have to show me how to do Little Joe when we get home," you say. It's as easy as that.

The Buddy yawns, says, "It's really easy."

"For you. I never could figure it out. Even when I was twice your age."

"Nuh-uh."

"Serious."

"Daddy," the Buddy says. "Grandpa said he showed you how to do it."

"He did," you say. "But I never really listened."

"Let's do it when we see momma." The Buddy yawns again.

"Another time," you say. "But I do want you to show me." You pause. The silence lengthens and you see green lights ahead. You clear your throat and say, "There are other tricks, too. We can Google some soon. But I used to love to watch your grandpa do Little Joe. It was like they weren't cards in his hands but little people, and what he said they did, it was like I could see it happening right there." You laugh a little drily, both at yourself for stalling so long at this simple task and at the kid you once were, watching.

"He'd be at a party and a table full of people would be watching him. I'd never be right next to him. I already knew the trick. Sort of. I wanted to see what the other people were doing when they watched him. And I wished I could be like him, Buddy, you know? Wished I could be as comfortable in my own skin as he was in his. Then Mom, your granny, would come by and she'd ask me what dad was doing. I'd tell her and she'd say, 'That old trick?' But she would smile and I think I even knew back then that they really loved each other, the way your mom and I do."

The soft snores from the back sound to your ears louder than they probably are. And in the rear view you can see that the Buddy's eyelids do not flutter. Only the most alarming of noises could disturb him, certainly not the sound of his father's own voice, his dad's own voice, finding itself in the telling. It would be easy to stop talking right now, James, for what good would it do? The intended audience might, at best, wake up tomorrow with memories of dreams of hearing a faint voice, the words distorted by distance. At worst, the Buddy will wake and have no memory whatsoever. But no matter. The story still hasn't found its ending yet. So start talking again, Jimmy. It's the best way to start dealing.

Dave Housley is the author of the story collections *If I Knew the Way, I Would Take You Home, Commercial Fiction* and *Ryan Seacrest is Famous*. He is one of the founding editors of *Barrelhouse* magazine, and a co-founder of the Conversations and Connections writer's conference. He lives in State College, PA, with his wife Lori and son Ben.

BL Pawelek is a dad, husband and hiker/runner/biker living in Minnesota. Other poetry collections include *Always/Siempre, So Hold Me Tight and Hold Me Tight* and *The Equation of Constants*. He tries to show mad love to everyone, especially you.

Ben Tanzer is the author of the books *My Father's House, You Can Make Him Like You, So Different Now, Orphans,* and *Lost in Space*, among others. He also oversees day-to-day operations of This Zine Will Change Your Life, directs publicity and content strategy for Curbside Splendor, and can be found online at This Blog Will Change Your Life, the center of his growing lifestyle empire.

Tom Willams is the author of two books of fiction: *The Mimic's Own Voice* and *Don't Start Me Talkin'*. He lives in Kentucky with his wife and their son.

Special Dedications

to Edward Shaw Alley
(on behalf of Henry Alley)

to James Campbell
(on behalf of Catherine Campbell)

to Raymond Denault
(on behalf of Phyllis Keating)

to Paul Jarvis
(on behalf of Cynthia Keating)

to Leo Leger
(on behalf of Dawn Leger)

to Ronald Pettus
(on behalf of Jason Pettus)

to Andrew Harrison Hollen, Jr.
(on behalf of Andrea Hollen)

Cobalt Press Benefactors

Special thanks to those who donated through our Kickstarter campaign.

Henry Alley
American Ninth Art Studios
Peter Anderson
Leah Angstman
David Atkinson
Ed Aymar
Robert Balun
Ellen Wade Beals
Blue Lyra Review
Jesse Bradley
James Brubaker
Catherine Cambell
Audrey Chin
Ian Chung
James Claffey
Comic Book Diner
Dan Coxon
Mark Cugini
Armey Dean
Lou Gaglia
Miguel Garcia
Shauna Gilligan
Steven Gowin
Edward Hamlin
Mike Hampton
Lori Hettler
Andrea Hollen
Dave Housley
Hayley Hughes
Sandra Hunter
Joshua Isard
Richard Jordan
Michelle Junot
Dave K
Todd Kaneko
Cynthia Keating
Phyllis Keating
Zoe Keating
Emily Kiernan
Philip Krummrich
Michael Landweber
Kevin Lavey
Dawn Leger
Steven Losco
Zachary Mann
Ryan McElroy
John McDermott
Dennis Must

benefactors continued...

Jenny O'Grady
Robert Peluso
Jason Pettus
Meredith Purvis
Danilo Quinonez
Allison Frase Reavis
Robin Naviasky Redding
Hugh Reynolds
Joseph Riippi
Rob Roensch
Seth Sawyers
Neil Serven
Lynn Simpson
JD Smith
Leslie Sussan
Ben Tanzer
An Tran
Erika Turner
Claudia Vergara
Alan Walowitz
Ronald Williams
Tom Williams
YesYes Books
Anonymous (3)

www.cobaltpress.org

www.ingramcontent.com/pod-product-compliance
Lightning Source LLC
Chambersburg PA
CBHW082123180726
48291CB00011B/2816

* 9 7 8 1 9 4 1 4 6 2 0 0 3 *